*REVOLUTIONARY PENNSYLVANIA SERIES*

I0107842

# The Outposts

## JOHN L. MOORE

SUNBURY
P R E S S

Mechanicsburg, PA  USA

Published by Sunbury Press, Inc.
Mechanicsburg, Pennsylvania

**www.sunburypress.com**

For information about special discounts for bulk purchases, please contact Sunbury Press Orders Dept. at (855) 338-8359 or orders@sunburypress.com.

To request one of our authors for speaking engagements or book signings, please contact Sunbury Press Publicity Dept. at publicity@sunburypress.com.

FIRST SUNBURY PRESS EDITION: October 2022

Set in Adobe Garamond | Interior design by Crystal Devine | Cover by Lawrence Knorr | Cover illustration: *Proofs of Our Courage* by Andrew Knez Jr. | Edited by Lawrence Knorr.

Publisher's Cataloging-in-Publication Data
Names: Moore, John L., author.
Title: The outposts / John L. Moore.
Description: First trade paperback edition. | Mechanicsburg, PA : Sunbury Press, 2020.
Summary: The Revolutionary War created conflict between Pennsylvanians and Virginians who settled in the Ohio River Valley and pro-British Indians who resisted the advent of white pioneers. The Outposts details events that occurred in 1777 through early 1779.
Identifiers: ISBN 979-8-88819-005-0 (softcover).
Subjects: HISTORY / United States / State & Local / Middle Atlantic | HISTORY / United States / Revolutionary Period.

Product of the United States of America
0  1  1  2  3  5  8  13  21  34  55

*Continue the Enlightenment!*

# Dedication

**For Uncle Harry**
When I was a boy, Uncle Harry (known to the rest of the world as Harry O. Evans, 1913–2003) took me to see the 1764 blockhouse at Fort Pitt in downtown Pittsburgh, Pennsylvania. My lifelong interest in the history of the Pennsylvania frontier dates to that visit.

Other books in the
Revolutionary Pennsylvania series:

*Murder at Killbuck Island*

*Against the Ice: The Story of December 1776*

*Tories, Terror, and Tea*

*Scorched Earth: General Sullivan and the Senecas*

*1780: Year of Revenge*

# Contents

# Acknowledgments

Jane E. Moore, Thomas Brucia, and Robert B. Swift read the manuscript and suggested improvements. Jane and Robert accompanied me on visits to many of the places mentioned in the narrative.

# Author's Note

I approach the many stories of the American Revolutionary War as a history-minded journalist. My mission lies in presenting the soldiers, civilians, and natives of the American frontier in their own words and in a way that lets modern readers experience a sense of immediacy with people who lived during the 1770s and 1780s. To accomplish this, I draw on soldiers' journals, letters, memoirs, and other first-person sources.

I have occasionally omitted phrases or sentences from quotations and have employed an ellipsis ( . . . ) to indicate where I have done so. In some instances, I have modernized spelling and punctuation.

## The word *squaw*

In writing about the American Frontier, one encounters a word that meant one thing in the 18th century but has taken on negative qualities in the centuries since. This is the word *squaw*. Merriam-Webster describes the word as offensive. According to Dictionary.com, it is a contemptuous term. Britannica.com says flatly, "The word *squaw* is very offensive and should be avoided."

Nevertheless, this word appears occasionally in *The Outposts*, nearly always within a direct quote. According to

John Heckewelder, the 18th-century Moravian missionary, *squaw* is derived from the Delaware word *ochqueu*, which in the 18th century simply meant woman. This is the meaning it has in these pages.

John L. Moore
Northumberland, Pennsylvania
September 2022

# Introduction

Soon after British soldiers and the American minute-men began shooting at each other in Massachusetts in 1775, the Continental Congress encouraged the Indians to be neutral.

"This is a family quarrel between us and Old England. You Indians are not concerned in it," the Congress said in a July 1775 speech addressed to the Haudenosaunee, also known as the Iroquois Confederacy. "We don't wish you to take up the hatchet against the king's troops. We desire you to remain at home, and not join on either side, but keep the hatchet buried deep . . . We desire to sit down under the same tree of peace with you."

The Congress also encouraged the Confederacy "to love peace and maintain it and to love and sympathize with us in our troubles." If the British ever asked the Iroquois to abandon their neutrality and "to join on their side, we only advise you to deliberate with great caution . . . for if the king's troops take away our property and destroy us who are of the same blood . . . what can you, who are Indians, expect from them afterward?"

Meeting in Philadelphia, the 2nd Continental Congress formally approved the text of this speech on July 13,

1775. It was addressed to "the Six Confederate Nations"—Mohawks, Oneidas, Tuscaroras, Onondagas, Cayugas, and Senecas—"from the Twelve United Colonies." The twelve were New Hampshire; Massachusetts Bay; Rhode Island; Connecticut; New York; New Jersey; Pennsylvania; the counties of New Castle, Kent, and Sussex on Delaware; Maryland; Virginia; North Carolina; and South Carolina."

Georgia wasn't listed. Although it eventually became the thirteenth colony to join the Congress, it did so too late for its name to appear on this document.

For a while, the Iroquois and many other Indian nations didn't take sides. In 1776, for instance, American officials and Shawnee and Delaware chiefs who attended a treaty at Fort Pitt heard Guyasuta, the Iroquois leader responsible for "the care of the Indians on the west side of the River Ohio," declare that the Six Nations intended to remain neutral.

Three hundred miles of Indian Country separated Fort Pitt, the American fort at the Forks of the Ohio, and Fort Detroit, a British post along the Detroit River near the western end of Lake Erie. "We will not suffer either the English or Americans to march an army through our country," said Guyasuta, also known as Kiashuta. He cautioned the Americans against mounting "an expedition against Detroit, for I repeat it to you again, we will not suffer an army to march through our country."

Many of the Ohio Indians were Delawares who had migrated west from eastern Pennsylvania and New Jersey earlier in the century. Shawnee bands that had once lived in central and eastern Pennsylvania had also moved to the region. The Iroquois claimed sovereignty over the land west of the Alleghenies and along the Ohio River and its tributaries by right of conquest of other tribes. The Shawnee and the Delaware settled there with permission from the Iroquois.

# It became '. . . dangerous to let a compass be seen'

By the mid-1700s, the descendants of the Lenni Lenape who had welcomed William Penn to the Delaware River Valley had come to distrust the white men who ventured into the Ohio and made surveys of their land.

Frontier surveyor Christopher Gist clearly understood the natives' attitude when in November 1750, he spent several days at Shannopin, a Delaware village located in what has become Pittsburgh. Shannopin, a village with about 20 families, was situated along the Allegheny River, about two miles above its confluence with the Monongahela River. "I was unwell and stayed in this town to recover," Gist said.

In his early 40s, Gist knew that practicing the surveyor's profession had become a risky business along the Ohio. Even so, "while I was here, I took an opportunity to set my compass privately, and took the distance across the river, for I understood it was dangerous to let a compass be seen among these Indians."

Gist was an agent of the Virginia-based Ohio Company. He had come to the Ohio River Valley with specific instructions: "When you find a large quantity of good, level land, such as you think will suit the company, you are to measure the breadth of it, in three or four different places, and take the courses of the river and mountains on which it binds in order to judge the quantity."

By November 25, Gist and the men in his party had reached Logstown, a native town inhabited chiefly by Delawares and Shawnee located along the Ohio about twenty miles below the confluence of the Monongahela and Allegheny rivers. "The people in this town began to enquire my business, and, because I did not readily inform them, they began to suspect me, and said I was come to settle the Indian's lands, and they knew I should never go home again safe," the surveyor wrote in his journal. Gist somehow evaded the danger.

These Delawares were the displaced descendants of Indians who had lived along the Delaware and lower Hudson rivers. They called themselves the Lenni Lenape, which meant "the original people." Early in the 18th century, they began moving west, first to the Susquehanna River Valley, then over the Alleghenies, and into the Ohio Valley.

Their ancestors had lost vast sections of their homeland to white land speculators, and they had come to associate the appearance of white men using compasses with the eventuality of being forced off their land. These natives objected vigorously when whites produced compasses and began to make surveys. To draw maps, Gist and other surveyors employed large compasses mounted on tripods.

On a subsequent trip in March 1752, Gist was approached by a Delaware Indian "who spoke good English." The man explained, "that . . . The Beaver and Captain Oppamylucah, . . . two chiefs of the Delawares, desired to know where the Indian's land lay, for . . . the French claimed all the land on one side the River Ohio and the English on the other side."

A century of dealing with white people had taught these Native Americans to be wary. During the 1600s, their ancestors had lived along what they called the *Lenapewihittuk,* or "Indian river," but is known today as the Delaware. They had lived close enough to the Atlantic Ocean to travel there to harvest shellfish every summer, but by the mid-1700s, most of the descendants of these Lenni Lenape, now referring to themselves as Delawares, lived hundreds of miles west of the ocean. European diseases had greatly reduced their numbers. European immigrants had acquired much of their land. As they moved—some, west; others, north—they became known by other names. For instance, when they lived along the Schuylkill River in southeastern Pennsylvania, the bands of which Sassoonan was chief were known as the "Schuylkill Indians." "Later, after they had sold all their land, and Sassoonan lived at Shamokin (present-day Sunbury), they were called 'Delawares of Shamokin,'" Paul Wallace said in his classic *The Indians of Pennsylvania.*

As the Delawares crossed the Allegheny Mountains during the early 1700s, white fur traders followed them. These traders came to sell their merchandise, not to settle. The native hunters and trappers welcomed them. The Indians needed the goods that traders hauled over the mountains in pack trains: guns, gunpowder, bullets, traps, knives, hatchets, tomahawks, scissors, shoes, shirts, coats, breeches, hats, buttons, beads, and rum. In turn, the traders wanted the beaver, deer, and bear pelts the Indians had to barter.

However, whites who arrived to establish homesteads didn't receive the same reception. By mid-century, the

Ohio Delawares made it clear that whites who came from Pennsylvania, Virginia, and other colonies to settle west of the Alleghenies weren't welcome.

As Ackowanothio, a Delaware chief who spoke on behalf of his people living along the Ohio, explained in 1758; the Indians had already sold all of their homelands in the Pennsylvania colony's eastern region. The whites there had had such a hunger for land that "where one of those people settled, like pigeons, a thousand more would settle." When the whites had bought up all the native lands, "we at last jumped over (the) Allegheny Hills, and settled on the waters of Ohio. Here we thought ourselves happy. We had plenty of game, a rich and large country, and a country that the Most High had created for the poor Indians, and not for the white people. How happy did we live here!"

But this happiness, Ackowanothio said, began to subside when the Indians learned that King George II of England had given the Ohio River Valley "to a parcel of covetous gentlemen from Virginia, called the Ohio Company, who came immediately and offered to build forts among us, no doubt, to make themselves master of our lands, and make slaves of us."

In 1754, French soldiers moved into the Ohio Valley and forced the Virginians to abandon a fort they were building at the confluence. The French built a fort of their own—Fort Duquesne—on the site the Virginians had picked. In 1758, a British army forced the French to evacuate the fort.

The Delawares quickly went on record that they didn't want the British to stay.

As Ackowanothio explained, French officers at Fort DuQuesne had warned the Ohio Indians that when whites from Virginia arrived in the Ohio Valley, "don't let them make the least settlement . . ." If permitted to stay, "they will in a few years settle the whole. They are as numerous as mosquitoes and gnats in the woods. If they get once a fast hold, it will not be in your power to drive them away again."

This caution struck the Delawares as reasonable. "We can drive away the French when we please," Ackowanothio told Conrad Weiser, the Pennsylvania official who recorded his remarks. ". . . We can never drive you off, you are such a numerous people, and that makes us afraid of your army . . ."

In early December, weeks after the French left, Delaware chiefs arrived at The Forks and met with Colonel Henry Bouquet, the British commander. "We have not come here to take possession of your hunting country in a hostile manner, . . . but to open a large and extensive trade with you," Bouquet said.

He explained that the British army would soon withdraw from the region. Even so, 200 men would remain "in order to protect our traders, and I can assure you that as soon as goods can be brought up, you will see a large trade opened for you." Bouquet asked, "you will treat those men . . . as your brethren, and support them, if in case the enemy should come and attempt to drive them away."

The response of the Delawares—delivered by The Beaver, a principal chief—made it

*Henry Bouquet, painted by John Wollaston circa 1760.*

clear that they would welcome traders from the English colonies. "We assure you it is agreeable to us." But while the Delawares would welcome English traders, The Beaver insisted that the Delawares didn't want a British fort on the Ohio.

The British disregarded this and soon began to build a fort they called Fort Pitt. The Delawares realized that it was larger than Fort Duquesne had been.

Pittsburgh sprang up a short distance away. By 1761, there were more than 100 dwellings in the village, according to James Kenny, a Pittsburgh storekeeper. He said his information about the town came from "a young man that was ordered by ye commanding officer, . . . to number all ye dwelling-houses without ye fort, marking the number on each door."

In 1763, an uprising led by Pontiac, an Ottawa war chief, saw Indians of many different midwestern tribes attack British posts and white settlements west of the Alleghenies. In Pennsylvania, Shawnee, Delaware, and Seneca warriors targeted Fort Pitt and three new British posts. At Presque' Isle on Lake Erie, for example, 200 warriors armed with guns and bows surrounded the fort on June 22 and began a two-day siege. They shot fire arrows over the walls and set the blockhouse ablaze.

Indians initiated hostilities at Fort Pitt on June 22. Two days later, a delegation of Delawares came to the fort and met with Captain Simeon Ecuyer, the commandant. The speaker, Turtle's Heart, told Ecuyer that he shouldn't be surprised that the warriors drove off the livestock and shot at the soldiers. He demanded the British abandon the post and return to the English settlements east of the mountains.

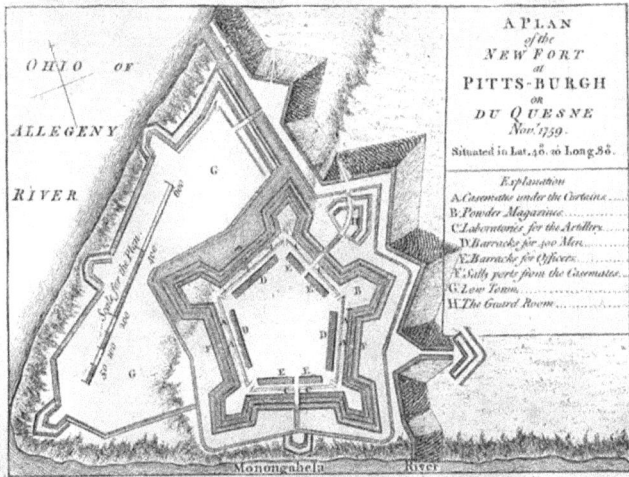

*1765 plan of Fort Pitt drawn by cartographer John Rocque.*

Ecuyer refused. When the Delawares said that a large force of native warriors would soon arrive to attack Fort Pitt, Ecuyer replied that two sizeable British armies were already marching to the frontier: 6,000 soldiers were headed to Fort Pitt, and 3,000 troops were bound for the Great Lakes. The captain was bluffing, but Turtle's Heart didn't know that.

As the meeting ended, the soldiers had a parting gift for the Delawares. "Out of our regard to them we gave them two blankets and a handkerchief out of the smallpox hospital." William Trent said. "I hope it will have the desired effect."

On July 26, the Delawares returned to the fort. Captain Ecuyer again met with a delegation that again insisted that the British should depart at once and return to the coastal colonies. If native forces attacked the post, "you yourselves are the cause of this," Turtle's Heart declared. "You marched your armies into our country, and built forts here, though we told you, again and again, that we wished you to remove. My brothers, this land is ours and not yours."

Ecuyer refused. "If any of you appear again about this fort, I will throw bombshells, which will burst and blow you to atoms, and fire cannon among you, loaded with a whole bag full of bullets," he warned.

Ultimately, the Indians failed to force the British to abandon Fort Pitt.

*Map of the Ohio Country.*

August 1772

# The British withdraw from Fort Pitt

A traveler who crossed Pennsylvania in 1772 chronicled the withdrawal of British troops from Fort Pitt. The details emerge from the journal that David McClure, a clergyman, kept while riding on horseback from Philadelphia to Pittsburgh and on into Ohio, which was then Indian territory.

On August 13, McClure and his companion, the Reverend Levi Frisbie, were in the Pennsylvania mountains, about 60 miles west of present-day Harrisburg, when they reached a remote hamlet that "contained only three or four log houses." The village stood along a military road that led over the Appalachian Mountains to Pittsburgh and the British stronghold of Fort Pitt.

The village's key feature was a minor military outpost, Fort Littleton, that the Pennsylvania colony had built 15 years earlier during the French and Indian War. "Here was a small guard of British soldiers, principally for the purposes of carrying dispatches from Fort Pitt to Philadelphia," McClure wrote. Fort Littleton was about 140 miles east of Pittsburgh and approximately 170 miles west of Philadelphia.

Recently ordained as Presbyterian ministers at Dartmouth College in New Hampshire, McClure and Frisbie had ridden hundreds of miles on horseback since leaving New Hampshire in mid-June. They wanted to establish a mission among the Delaware Indians living in Ohio.

The next day—August 14—the travelers met a formidable challenge in crossing another mountain. Although they rode most of the way, they walked behind their horses at least part of the time. In ascending the ridge, they found "some parts so steep that we were necessitated to hold by the tails of our horses and let them haul us up," McClure said. He and Frisbie had to continually watch the feet of their horses, so they weren't "wounded by the stones, which their feet threw back upon us."

McClure noted that late in the day, they met a detachment of British soldiers from Fort Pitt escorting an east-bound pack train—"15 horses carrying cannon balls"—from Fort Pitt to Philadelphia.

On August 15, the clergymen "ascended a steep hill, and, descending a valley, came to Stony Creek," a stream east of the Westmoreland County settlement of Ligonier. Along the way that day, McClure and Frisbie "met two soldiers express from Fort Pitt (going) to General (Thomas) Gage," the British commander-in-chief who had headquarters in New York.

It was sunset on August 19 when Frisbie and McClure reached Fort Pitt, which McClure described as "a handsome and strong fortification." The fort stood on the point of land where the Allegheny and Monongahela rivers join to form the Ohio River. "Adjoining are a good orchard and gardens," he said. There were barracks for the soldiers, "comfortable houses," presumably for the officers, and "one large brick house, called the Governor's House."

Built in 1758, Fort Pitt had served as a key Ohio River defense for nearly 13 years., By 1772, the Indian wars had been over for eight years, and the British high command saw little need for retaining the post. McClure and Frisbie would have been unaware of this as they rode into town.

The village of Pittsburgh—"about 40 dwelling houses made of hewed logs"—stood along the Monongahela about a quarter mile southeast of the fort. McClure characterized the village as "the headquarters of Indian traders, and the resort of Indians of different and distant tribes who come to exchange their peltry and furs for rum, blankets, and ammunition."

On Sunday, August 23, at the invitation of the commandant, Major Hamilton, McClure preached to the Fort Pitt garrison in the morning. "In the afternoon, Mr. Frisbie preached in the village. A great part of the people here make the Sabbath a day of recreation, drinking, and profanity."

McClure painted a dismal picture of the town: "The inhabitants of this place are very dissipated. They seem to feel themselves beyond the arm of government and freed from the restraining influence of religion. It is the resort of Indian traders, and many here have escaped from justice and from creditors in the old settlements.

"The greater part of the Indian traders keep a squaw, and some of them a white woman, as a temporary wife."

Before the missionaries were ready to leave Pittsburgh, Frisbie fell ill and went to Fort Pitt to see the medical officer, a young Irish physician named Dr. Edward Hand. Hand examined Frisbie and advised against his "going into the Indian Country."

Traveling into Ohio without Frisbie, McClure retained a frontiersman named Joseph Nickels as his companion and hired a Delaware Indian, Joseph Pepee, as an interpreter. Their destination was a populous Delaware town about 100 miles due west of Pittsburgh. It was located along the Tuscarawas, a branch of the Muskingum, which, in turn, was a tributary of the Ohio.

The chief was an elderly Delaware, Netawatwees, known among the English as Newcomer. "This town is called Newcomers Town by the English," McClure noted.

He counted "about 60 houses, some of logs, and others the bark of trees, fastened by elm bark to poles stuck in the ground and bent over at the top. There are nearly 100 families." He noted that "some of the houses are well built, with hewed logs, with stone chimneys, chambers, and cellars. These I was told were built by the English captives, in the time of the French wars."

Newcomerstown was an agricultural community. "Eight or 10 acres around the town are cleared. On the opposite side of the river is a large cornfield in rich low ground. It is enclosed within one common fence, and each family has its division to plant."

The clergyman formally asked the chief for permission to teach Christianity to the villagers and then waited several weeks for the chief's reply. While he waited, "news arrived that the British troops were dismantling Fort Pitt, and were about to leave the country," he reported.

This was a welcome development at Newcomerstown. "The warriors could not conceal their joy at this event," McClure said. "The fort had been a bridle upon them hitherto, to restrain their murders and depredations on the frontiers."

Chief Newcomer and his councilors eventually rejected McClure's request and politely informed him of this during a formal meeting. McClure replied, "that I was very sorry that they had rejected an offer intended for their greatest good . . . I mentioned that it was our intention to have procured a school master to instruct their children, and also to furnish them some utensils for husbandry, and a grist mill."

McClure's remarks irritated at least one of Newcomer's councilors. "One of them, with expressions of anger, said they did not like that the white people should settle upon the Ohio," the clergyman said. "They destroyed their hunting."

When he returned to Pittsburgh on October 19, Mc-Clure found significant change at Fort Pitt. "In consequence of orders from General Gage, the garrison are preparing to

*This blockhouse was built in 1764 as part of Fort Pitt. (1902 photo)*

depart," he wrote. "They have begun to destroy the fortress. This is a matter of surprise and grief to the people around, who have requested that the fortress may stand as a place of security to them" in the event of an Indian uprising.

Curious as to why the British were demolishing the works, "I asked one of the officers, the reason of their destroying a fort, so necessary to the safety of the frontiers? He replied, 'The Americans will not submit to the British Parliament, and they may now defend themselves.'"

Levi Frisbie had recovered by the time McClure returned to Pittsburgh. For many months, the missionaries remained in western Pennsylvania to minister to pioneers who had settled west of the Alleghenies, where churches were few. On November 17, as McClure was riding from Ligonier to Pittsburgh, he encountered an east-bound convoy of "soldiers and wagons loaded with ammunition, etcetera, going to Philadelphia." It had left Fort Pitt a few days earlier. These troops were among the last to leave the fort.

# Virginia seizes control of Pittsburgh, Fort Pitt

The British withdrawal from Fort Pitt in late 1772 created a political crisis for Pittsburgh and the vicinity. The Pennsylvania colony officially regarded the village and the area around it as part of Westmoreland County, which it had created in 1773. But the governor of Virginia—John Murray, the 4th Earl of Dunmore—wanted the region for his colony.

In creating the new county, Pennsylvania transferred western sections of Bedford County to Westmoreland. The change saw The Forks placed within the new jurisdiction, which had its county seat at Hannastown, about 35 miles due east of Pittsburgh along the road that linked Pittsburgh and Philadelphia. The new government quickly organized, "with 16 magistrates . . . appointed to administer justice within its boundaries," according to Edgar W. Hassler in his 1900 book, *Old Westmoreland: A History of Western Pennsylvania During the Revolution*.

Topping the list of magistrates was the name of William Crawford, the land speculator and business associate of George Washington. Crawford had previously served as a magistrate when Governor John Penn and Pennsylvania's

*A reconstruction of the governor's palace at Williamsburg, Virginia. (Photo by Robert B. Swift)*

Provincial Council created Bedford County in March 1771. Originally from Virginia, Crawford had settled at a village called Stewart's Crossing on the Youghiogheny River, a tributary of the Monongahela River. Known today as Connellsville, it was about 45 miles south of Pittsburgh.

Pennsylvania's creation of a civil government for the Forks of the Ohio didn't sit well in Williamsburg, the capital of Virginia. "These proceedings stirred up the Virginia authorities," Hassler says. Governor Murray, better known as Lord of Dunmore, soon "took forcible possession of the disputed territory." The governor appointed Pittsburgh resident John Connolly as commandant at Pittsburgh. "Connolly mustered the militia under Virginia law, seized and garrisoned Fort Pitt, intimidated the Pennsylvania magistrates, marched some of them off to prison, and established the authority of Virginia throughout all the

*Replica of a colonial wagon at Williamsburg, Virginia. (Photo by Robert B. Swift)*

region between the Monongahela and the Ohio," Hassler reports. "Pennsylvania, having no militia law, was power-less to resist . . ."

On January 1, 1774, Connolly posted public notices in Pittsburgh and several other settlements in the region: Lord Dunmore "has been pleased to nominate and appoint me captain, commandant of the Militia of Pittsburgh and its dependencies." Also, the governor realizes "the necessity of erecting a new (Virginia) county to include Pittsburgh."

As militia commander, Connolly declared, "I hereby require and command all persons in the Dependency of Pittsburgh, to assemble themselves there as a militia on the 25th instant, at which time I shall communicate other matters for the promotion of public utility."

By springtime, Connolly had his militia strengthening the defenses of Fort Pitt, which he renamed Fort Dunmore.

Although Pennsylvania objected to Connolly's actions, Pittsburgh and Fort Pitt functioned as Virginia territory for the next year and a half.

## Dunmore, Crawford lead the Virginia militia against the Shawnee

In 1774, Lord Dunmore led an expedition against the Shawnees and Mingos living west of the Ohio. He left Williamsburg in July, bound for the Shawnee towns west of the Ohio River hundreds of miles below Pittsburgh. Moving slowly, he crossed the Alleghenies to reach Fort Dunmore at Pittsburgh. From there, in late September, Dunmore sailed 110 miles downriver to Wheeling in present-day West Virginia, where Crawford had built Fort Fincastle in June. "His Lordship arrived here yesterday with about 1,200 men, 700 of whom came by water with his Lordship, and 500 came, under my brother William, by land," Valentine Crawford told George Washington in an October 1 letter written at Fort Fincastle. Crawford's responsibilities included driving a herd of cattle that served as a source of fresh meat for the troops.

At one point, Dunmore sent Crawford ahead to meet a second army from Virginia, this one commanded by Colonel Andrew Lewis, that was advancing on the Ohio. According to Valentine Crawford, "His Lordship has sent him with 500 men, 50 pack-horses, and 200 bullocks (steers), to meet Colonel Lewis, at the mouth of Hockhocking, below the mouth of the Little Kanawha."

The Hockhocking, which drains a section of southern Ohio, is known today as the Little Hocking River.

*1772 portrait depicts George Washington as a
Virginia officer during the French and Indian War,
by Charles Willson Peale.*

The confluence of the two rivers was 225 miles below
Fort Pitt. After meeting Lewis, William Crawford was "to
build a stockade fort, or a large block-house, . . . below the
mouth of the Kanawha. His Lordship is to go by water
with the rest of the troops in a few days," Valentine Crawford said.

This fort, which would have been constructed on land
owned by Washington, wasn't ever built. Instead, Crawford
crossed the Ohio and erected a fort at the confluence of
the Hockhocking and the Ohio. The Hockhocking is now

called the Hocking. The stockade post, which Lord Dunmore named Fort Gower to honor a British politician, was
located at present-day Hockingport, Ohio.

Before Lord Dunmore could reach him, Lewis fought
the Shawnees at modern Point Pleasant. Both sides had
heavy losses, and Lewis was killed. As the fighting ended,
the Indians retreated west across the Ohio, then withdrew
inland, apparently headed for their principal settlement,
Chillicothe, on the Scioto River about 100 miles due west
of present-day Parkersburg, West Virginia.

As Lord Dunmore entered the region, the Shawnee
decided to make peace. The treaty they signed with Virginia had strict terms. "First, they have to give up all the
prisoners taken ever by them in war with white people; also
negroes and all the horses stolen or taken by them since the
last war." William Crawford later told Washington. "And

*The Westmoreland Historical Society has recreated Hannastown, the
county seat of Pennsylvania's Westmoreland County created in 1773.
The county originally included Pittsburgh.*

*Hannastown historic marker.*

further, no Indian for the future is to hunt on the east side of the Ohio, nor any white man on the west side; as that seems to have been the cause of some of the disturbance between our people and them." To guarantee "that they will perform their part of the agreement, they have given up four chief men, to be kept as hostages," Crawford said.

When the Mingos refused to make peace, the governor sent Crawford, who now held the rank of major, to attack them. "Lord Dunmore ordered myself with 240 men to set out in the night. We were to march to a town about 40 miles distant from our camp, up the Scioto, where we understood the whole of the Mingos were to rendezvous upon the following day." The Indians intended "to slip off while we were settling matters with the Shawnee." They planned to travel hurriedly to Lake Erie "and take their prisoners with them and their horses which they had stolen."

Stealth became a key to Crawford's strategy. "We marched out . . . under pretense of going to Hockhocking for more provisions. Few knew of our setting off anyhow, and none knew where we were going to until the next day. Our march was performed with as much speed as possible. We arrived at a town called the Salt-Lick Town the ensuing night, and at daybreak we got around it with one-half our force, and the remainder were sent to a small village half a mile distant."

The strategy succeeded. "The whole of the Mingos were ready to start, and were to have set out the morning we attacked them," Crawford reported.

The major's troops lost the element of surprise when a militia soldier "creeping up to" the Mingo camp came upon a warrior laying alongside a log some distance from the Indian town. "This obliged the man to kill the Indian." The incident made so much noise that many Mingos got away. Even so, the Virginians killed six Indians, wounded a number of others and took 14 prisoners. "We got all their baggage and horses, 10 of their guns, and 200 white prisoners," Crawford said. When the militia returned to the settlements, "the plunder sold for 400 pounds sterling."

## 1775: Connolly abruptly leaves The Forks

In 1775, soon after the outbreak of the Revolutionary War, Captain Connolly's reign at Fort Dunmore ended nearly as suddenly as it had begun. A Loyalist, Connolly saw his popularity plunge as revolutionary fervor swept through the frontier settlements. News of New England forces fighting the British in Massachusetts, first at Lexington and Concord in April and then at Bunker Hill at Boston two months later, electrified Virginia and Pennsylvania residents along the Ohio.

Connolly's fate at The Forks was tied to Lord Dunmore's. The governor, a staunch Loyalist himself, encountered such rebellious sentiment in Virginia that he fled Williamsburg and, "now driven for personal safety," took refuge aboard a British ship off Norfolk, Connolly said later.

When Connolly learned that Dunmore was both living and attempting to govern the colony from the safety of a warship, he left The Forks. The Continental Army eventually assumed control of the Ohio Valley. The fort was renamed Fort Pitt, and Pennsylvania's Westmoreland County resumed governing Pittsburgh.

After teaming up with Lord Dunmore off the Virginia coast, Connolly hatched a plan to organize an army consisting of British soldiers from Detroit and Canada as well as Loyalists from the Ohio Valley. These troops would act in concert "with Indian auxiliaries"—mainly Delaware warriors from Ohio. This strike force would march east from the Ohio Valley in early 1776 and join Loyalist soldiers led by Dunmore at Alexandria, Virginia.

Headed for Detroit to organize this expedition, Connolly was traveling across Maryland in November 1775 when the local organization of Minute Men arrested him and his companions at an inn near Hagerstown. "About 2 o'clock in the morning they suddenly broke into the room where we lay, and made us prisoners," Connolly said later. He and his companions were taken to Hagerstown, where the Committee of Safety interrogated them. A search of Connolly's baggage turned up a copy of his plan to invade Virginia.

Connolly's jailers soon transferred him to Pennsylvania. According to the April 6, 1776, minutes of the Committee of Safety in Philadelphia, John Connolly was "a prisoner in the jail of this county" and described as "dangerous to the safety of America."

The American government kept Connolly imprisoned for much of the war.

# Militia wouldn't stop killing friendly Delawares

Six months after taking command at Fort Pitt on June 1, 1777, Brigadier General Edward Hand concluded that the Western Department needed regular soldiers from the Continental Army, not militia. Hand realized that the militia troops he was forced to rely on were undisciplined, undependable, violent, and even murderous. "I had rather resign my office than continue here in command of militia," Hand said in a December 24, 1777 letter written to Richard Peters, secretary of the U.S. Board of War.

In September, as Hand had settled into his new post, he saw that the manpower available to him included a small assortment of regular soldiers from the Continental Army: a detachment of men from the 13th Virginia Regiment as well as "a few stragglers and deserters from the 8th Pennsylvania and other regiments." But these men were too few to help him reach his objectives.

*General Edward Hand*

To do that, he was forced to rely on militia troops from Pennsylvania and Virginia.

"The western Indians are united against us," Hand told General Washington in a September 15 letter. To counter this, Hand had begun organizing "an expedition that must . . . be carried in to the Indian Country" west of the Ohio River. In late summer, he called out the militia, hoping to assemble an army large enough to strike the pro-British tribes whose fighters had been raiding white settlements along the Ohio and Allegheny.

"But, alas! I was disappointed," Hand told General Washington on November 9. Too few militia troops turned out, and the plan fell through. "The whole force I was able to collect . . . did not exceed 800 men. I am therefore obliged to content myself with stationing small detachments on the frontiers to prevent as much as possible the inroads of the savages."

Writing from Fort Pitt, Hand said he was about to leave Pittsburgh on a trip downriver to Fort Henry at present-day Wheeling, West Virginia, and then on to Fort Randolph at modern Point Pleasant, also in West Virginia, "to establish some order at these posts."

This remark turned out to be an understatement. When Hand reached Fort Randolph several days later, he learned that Virginia militia soldiers had several days earlier murdered three Shawnee chiefs being held there as hostages.

The dead included Cornstalk, an important Shawnee chief who had recently come to Fort Randolph on a visit. During the visit, Cornstalk told the commandant, Captain Matthew Arbuckle, "that he was opposed to joining the war on the side of the British, but that all the rest of the

(Shawnee) nation . . . were determined to engage in it." As another officer, Captain John Stuart, reported later, Cornstalk explained that if all the other Shawnee went over to the British, "he should have to run with the stream (as he expressed it) on which Captain Arbuckle thought proper to detain him, the young Redhawk and another fellow as hostages to prevent the nation from joining the British."

The killings happened on November 10. The three chiefs, along with Cornstalk's son, Elinipsico, were all locked in a cabin inside the fort when two Virginia militiamen left the militia camp without permission to go hunting across from the fort, which overlooked the confluence of the Ohio and Kanawha rivers.

The two soldiers—Robert Gilmore and a man named Hamilton—had crossed the Kanawha unaware that hostile warriors were lurking in brush along the riverbank and spying on the fort. As the soldiers returned from hunting, Gilmore stumbled on the Indians who shot him.

Captain John Stuart said afterward that he and Captain Matthew Arbuckle were "standing on the opposite bank" when they heard the gunshot. The officers "wondered what anyone was doing there firing contrary to orders."

Immediately after this, they saw Hamilton run down the bank "and call out that Gilmore was killed."

Stuart saw several men in Gilmore's company rush down to the river where they "jumped in to a canoe, and went to the relief of Hamilton" on the Kanawha's opposite shore. They rescued Hamilton, then "brought the corpse of Gilmore down the bank, scalped and covered with blood."

As the soldiers returned to the Fort Randolph side of the river, "the cry was raised, 'Let us kill the Indians in the fort,' and every man with his gun in his hand came up the bank pale as death with rage," Stuart reported. Identifying the company commander as Captain John Hall, Stuart said that "Captain Hall was at their head."

Stuart and Arbuckle attempted to stop the soldiers, "but they cocked their guns, threatened us with instant death if we did not desist, and rushed into the fort," Stuart said.

Inside, the soldiers hurried to the cabin where the Indians were confined. "The men advanced to the door," Stuart said. "The Cornstalk arose and met them. Seven or eight bullets were fired into him, and his son was shot dead as he sat upon a stool." The other Shawnee chiefs were also killed.

In his report to the Board of War, General Hand emphasized that the killing occurred "notwithstanding Captain Arbuckle's endeavors to prevent it."

Hand understood that the murder of a chief who opposed siding with the British would push his people entirely away from the Americans. "We have little reason to expect a reconciliation with the Shawnees," he wrote.

Born and educated in Ireland, Hand studied medicine at Trinity College in Dublin. He was in his early 20s when he joined the 18th Royal Irish Infantry as a surgeon's mate. In 1767, the regiment was sent to North America. It spent several years at Fort Pitt and withdrew to eastern Pennsylvania after the British abandoned the fort in 1772.

Hand left the military around 1774 and settled in Lancaster, Pennsylvania, where he established a medical practice before the outbreak of the Revolution. When the war started, Hand's army experience proved valuable. He served at Boston in 1775 as the lieutenant colonel of a battalion of Pennsylvania riflemen. He was promoted to brigadier general before traveling west and taking command at Fort Pitt.

As 1777 ended, intelligence arrived at Fort Pitt that British forces from Fort Detroit had stored a quantity of military supplies at a native village along the Cuyahoga River in eastern Ohio at present-day Akron. The village was along an important Indian trail, the Mahoning Path, that linked the Sandusky and Ohio rivers. On December 28, Hand wrote to Colonel William Crawford: "There are at Cuyahoga about 100 miles from here, a magazine of arms and provisions sent from Detroit, and 15 bateaux lie there. You may guess the rest."

Hand determined to destroy these supplies. On February 5, he advised Crawford, ". . . I am credibly informed that the English have lodged a quantity of arms, ammunition, provision, and clothing at a small Indian town, about 100 miles from Fort Pitt." The British wanted the Indians to draw on these materials "in their excursions against the inhabitants of" the American settlements along the Ohio and Allegheny Rivers.

Hand wanted to prevent this. "I ardently wish to collect as many brave, active lads as are willing to turn out to destroy this magazine," he told Crawford. "Every man must be provided with a horse, and every article necessary to equip them for the expedition, except ammunition, which, with some arms, I can furnish."

Although it was winter, Hand told Crawford that he wouldn't wait for spring weather before setting out. "I . . . expect that you will use your influence on this occasion, and bring all the volunteers you can raise to Fort Pitt by the 15th of this month."

Decades later, a volunteer named Samuel Murphy told an interviewer he remembered that when General Hand's strike force left Pittsburgh in mid-February, there had been "a slight fall of fresh snow."

A scant three weeks later, General Hand had returned to Fort Pitt, where he reflected on how miserably the expedition had failed. In a March 7 letter to a friend, Hand reported that he had led an expedition of nearly 500 soldiers—"chiefly Westmoreland Militia"—down the Ohio to the Beaver River, then up the Beaver and past present-day New Castle, Pennsylvania. He intended to swing west along the Mahoning Path and accomplish his "project of seizing them by surprise, during the season in which the savages might suppose us to be inactive."

Adverse weather soon complicated Hand's plan. "Unluckily," he wrote, "the heavy rains that fell soon after we set out, together with the melting of the snow, raised the waters to such a degree that, after swimming some creeks and going round the heads of others, we were obliged to relinquish our design."

Around this time, the soldiers were about 40 miles up the Beaver when they discovered Indian tracks. The general sent out scouts to see what lay ahead.

"Some of them returned and informed (that) they had found a camp containing between 50 and 60 Indians," Hand said. "I conjectured they were warriors coming into our settlements and proceeded to attack them, but to my great mortification (the soldiers) found only one man with some women and children." The militia troops "were so impetuous that I could not prevent their killing the man and one of the women. Another woman was taken and with difficulty saved. The remainder escaped."

Samuel Murphy, the elderly veteran, recalled additional details: The fighting occurred around mid-day on snow-covered ground. As the militia approached the town, "orders had been given . . . to surround it," but the soldiers left a gap through which a woman and children escaped. An elderly woman "was pursued and shot at repeatedly." A Virginian ran up to her "and tried to pull her away," but wasn't able to do so, "the bullets still flying." At this point, "a major came up and put a stop to firing, when it was ascertained that the only injury she had received was the loss of an end of a little finger."

Lieutenant John Hamilton of the 13th Virginia spotted another old woman and, "mistaking her for a warrior," shot her in the leg, Murphy said. Just then, "a soldier ran up and tomahawked her, and a second ran up and shot her."

Vastly outnumbered, the Indians nonetheless attempted to defend themselves. Murphy recalled that the sole native man in the camp had "shot and wounded Captain (David) Scott and disabled his arm." The Indian was "nearly ready to shoot again" when a soldier shot him, and a militia captain, Reasin Virgin, "sunk the tomahawk in his head."

"Then commenced a wild yelling and shooting, without giving the least heed to the officers," Murphy said.

When the soldiers eventually stopped shooting, they looted the camp's few cabins and collected "a little plunder," Murphy said.

General Hand and the other soldiers had no way of knowing it at the time, but the man they killed happened to be the brother of Captain Pipe, an important Delaware chief. Pipe said later that Hand's troops had also killed an unspecified number of his other relatives.

Hand's situation continued to deteriorate as the day wore on. As her captors interrogated her, the elderly woman who survived the attack told the soldiers that 10 miles upstream, 10 Munsey men were making salt.

"I detached a party to secure them," the general said. "They turned out to be four women and a boy. Of these, one woman only was saved."

In detailing his memories of these events decades later, the volunteer Murphy said it was the night before the soldiers reached the Munsey camp, which he said was "up the Mahoning at a place called the Salt Licks." They found only a few women. ". . . The warriors (were) all absent hunting," Murphy said. The soldiers took one woman as a captive and left the others.

During this episode, "a small Indian boy out with a gun shooting birds was discovered and killed," Murphy said. "Several claimed the honor." To settle the dispute, a scout named Simon Girty did some informal fact-finding and determined that a militia soldier named Zachariah Connell had "killed the lad."

Back at Fort Pitt, General Hand quickly realized that the expedition up the Beaver reflected poorly on his leadership. Not only had he failed to destroy the British supply depot on the Cuyahoga, but he had also led unprovoked attacks on the camps of friendly Delaware and Munsey Indians. They belonged to tribes that were formally allied with the Americans. Hand asked the Continental Congress to recall him.

In the March 7 letter, the general acknowledged the "savage conduct" of his troops. Written to Jasper Yeates, a Lancaster lawyer who happened to be the uncle of Hand's wife, the letter described the atrocities committed against the women.

He gave Yeates a detailed account of the attacks on the Delaware camps. "You will be surprised in performing the above great exploits, I had but one man (a captain) wounded, and one drowned," he said.

That same day, March 7, Hand also wrote to Colonel David Shepherd, the militia commander at Fort Henry downriver at Wheeling. Hand blamed his failure to destroy the Cuyahoga magazine on "the badness of the weather and height of the waters" and suggested that a force of 200 "Virginia gentlemen" might attack the depot in early spring. Such a venture "should meet my hearty concurrence," he said.

The general disclosed that he himself was contemplating "penetrating the enemy's country in May." He asked the colonel to share "your sentiments on the subject."

Replying several days later, the colonel was supportive without being definite. He noted that militia troops from Virginia's interior regions were leaving Wheeling, where they had been on temporary duty. "They are all returning home to tell of the great exploits they have done on the Ohio," Shepherd said dourly. ". . . I hope they will send us better men the next time."

On May 2, 1778, the Continental Congress accepted Hand's criticisms of the frontier militia. In recalling him, it authorized the creation of two new regiments "for the protection and operation on the Western Frontiers." The new outfits would consist of 12 companies of soldiers from Virginia and four companies from Pennsylvania. The men would each serve for a full year.

In approving Hand's recall, Congress also resolved that "General Washington be desired to appoint the officer to take the command at Fort Pitt." Hand remained at Pittsburgh until General Lachlan McIntosh, a Georgian who had spent the winter at Valley Forge, arrived in early August to succeed him.

The records show that before McIntosh reached his new post, the Indian agent at Fort Pitt, Colonel George Morgan, submitted a blistering summary of Hand's misadventure on the Beaver to the Board of War. Morgan's comments were part of a much longer letter, dated July 17, on another topic. Nonetheless, the agent reported that "last winter 500 or 600 men went from Fort Pitt and could find no hostile Indians, but they killed Captain Pipe's brother, a noted friend to the United States; two Indian squaws and a little boy; and took two squaws prisoners, all Delawares who in confidence of our friendship were seated about 45 miles from Fort Pitt, making salt and hunting for skins."

In September, a delegation of Delawares came to Fort Pitt for a weeklong treaty that formally renewed the bonds of friendship between the Delawares and the Americans. The minutes list Captain Pipe as one of the three principal chiefs.

Three months after this, Captain Pipe sent a message to McIntosh, apparently accompanied by a string of white wampum, emphasizing that "the loss of my relations who were killed last spring at the Salt Licks" hadn't prompted him to go over to the British.

"My heart is good," the chief told McIntosh. He added, "I never meant to quit the hold I have of the friendship subsisting between us."

The Pipe, also known as Hopocan, added: "If you are desirous of speaking of the loss of my friends, who were killed at the Salt Licks, there is a great many of my relations at Cooshackung (present-day Coshocton, Ohio). Your speaking to them will answer the same end as speaking to me."

Pipe's message took a roundabout route to reach McIntosh. He made the remarks in a conversation with another Delaware chief, Captain Killbuck. In turn, Killbuck dictated them to Colonel John Gibson at Fort Laurens on December 21. Gibson wrote them down and enclosed them in a letter he was writing to General McIntosh.

# Delawares to let Americans cross Indian Country

Button Gwinnett's star shone brightly in 1776. He signed the Declaration of Independence as a Georgia delegate to the 2nd Continental Congress. But in 1777, his star flamed out.

That's when Gwinnett ran afoul of Lachlan McIntosh, a brigadier general in the Continental Army responsible for protecting southern Georgia from British forces based in Florida. An action Gwinnett took while acting governor of Georgia angered McIntosh, who publicly denounced him as "a scoundrel and lying rascal."

Gwinnett challenged McIntosh to a duel. The two faced off with pistols at 12 paces in a pasture near Savannah on May 16. Each fired and wounded the other. McIntosh recovered, but Gwinnett died three days later.

The next 12 months proved hectic for McIntosh, a middle-aged Scot who had emigrated to Georgia as a child. Following Gwinnett's death, Georgia authorities tried McIntosh, an experienced military commander in his early 50s, for murder. He was acquitted.

Months later, General Washington, acting at the request of a congressman from Georgia, brought McIntosh to Pennsylvania and gave him command of the North Carolina Brigade at Valley Forge.

*Button Gwinnett*            *General Lachlan McIntosh*

In May 1778, Washington appointed the general to "command at Fort Pitt and in the Western Frontiers." In mid-summer, McIntosh headed west across the Allegheny Mountains, bound for Pittsburgh. He arrived in Pittsburgh on August 6 and relieved General Edward Hand.

News of McIntosh's new assignment crossed the frontier a month before he did. On July 8, a Virginia officer, Colonel William Christian, wrote to a friend that "an expedition is ordered against the Northwestern Indians and Detroit. The army to consist of 500 regulars and 2,500 militia. The whole to be commanded by General McIntosh of Georgia, a brigadier in the Continental Army."

By the time McIntosh reached Pittsburgh, the British had already held a treaty at Fort Detroit. In June, Governor Henry Hamilton welcomed representatives of the Ottawa, Chippewa, Huron, Potawatomi, and Miami nations at Detroit. At least one Delaware chief, Captain James, took part, but top-ranking Delaware chiefs didn't attend.

Hamilton's session produced a written message "sent from the war and village chiefs" of the pro-British tribes to the absent Delawares. Dated June 18, it complained that warriors allied with Hamilton occasionally found their trail blocked when passing Delaware towns in central Ohio on their way to raid white settlements in Virginia and Pennsylvania.

"They have sometimes found branches and other obstacles in their war path. We . . . observe you break the branches from the trees to put in the road," the chiefs said. "We . . . want to know why the warriors path has been stopped. We believe you to be the authors of it. This is the sentiments of all the war chiefs . . ."

The pro-British chiefs admonished the Delawares to break with the Americans and to join Governor Hamilton "and obey his will."

For his part, Hamilton reported that Captain James, a Delaware chief who did attend the treaty, had accepted the governor's tomahawk on behalf of the Delawares. Accompanying the weapon was a belt of wampum for the Delawares. "Hold it fast," Hamilton told Captain James, "Be wise, and remember that this belt I give you repeats the words of all the war chiefs and village chiefs present this day."

Hamilton's actions troubled Coquetageghton (White Eyes), a prominent Delaware chief who was a firm friend and ally of the United States. White Eyes had been an influential chief during the last years of the elderly Netawatwes (Newcomer), who died in 1776. Influential after Gelelemend (also known as Captain Killbuck) succeeded Newcomer as principal chief, White Eyes remained instrumental in keeping the tribe neutral when some other Delaware chiefs wanted to go over to the British. One consequence was that the pro-British tribes had expressed anger toward White Eyes at Fort Detroit during the summer of 1778.

"The nations have agreed to fall upon the Delawares, and the Wyandots are to make the beginning," White Eyes said in a July 19 letter to Colonel George Morgan, the Indian agent at Fort Pitt. "It is always said that we shall not listen to the singing birds, but now I have listened to them, because I believe it to be true."

White Eyes lived at or near the Delaware town of Goschachking (present-day Coshocton, Ohio), where the Tuscarawas joins the Walhonding River to form the Muskingum. He told Morgan that two Delaware warriors had stopped at Goschachking on their way home from the Detroit treaty and had warned him. These men "saw the tom(a)hawk handed to all the nations, and it was also given to them to carry it to me, which I have now to expect soon. It was told at the same time that whosoever would not take the tom(a)hawk . . . should be whipped."

The tension between the Delaware Nation and the other Mid-Western tribes was hardly new. Earlier in the war, news that the Iroquois, Wyandots, and some Shawnees intended to fight against the Americans had disturbed the Delawares.

"The chief Netawatwes, together with the chiefs White Eyes, Gelelemend, (alias Killbuck) Machingwi Puschiis, (alias the Big cat,) and others did every thing in their power to preserve peace among the nations," said the Reverend John Heckewelder, another Moravian missionary who then lived near Goschachking. These chiefs exhorted the other Indians "not to take up the hatchet or to join either side," Heckewelder said, but "the Sandusky Wyandots insolently . . . advised their cousins (the Delawares) to keep good shoes in readiness for to join the warriors."

In the aftermath of the Detroit treaty, White Eyes saw the seriousness of his predicament. "If I should not take the tom(a)hawk, they would try to force me to it, and now the time cometh that they will do this," he told Colonel Morgan. "Therefore, I desire you to . . . assist me."

Over time, White Eyes had proved his friendship to the Americans at Fort Pitt, in part by providing Morgan with intelligence. Pro-British Indians eventually realized that he was doing this and now held it against him. "They say that I tell you all what passeth when warriors go by here or that they heard I had been at the fort," he said. "I am blamed by the nations that I betray them, therefore keep all what I tell you secret."

The chief warned Morgan that their foes might monitor traffic between Goschachking and Pittsburgh. "We are afraid that the road between us is watched by the warriors and therefore not safe for messengers to travel," he said. He suggested that "should you want to send a message to me some time hence, then appoint a day, time, and place where our and your messengers are to meet one another."

He advised Morgan against sending messengers from Fort Pitt directly to Goschachking. "It is very dangerous for your messengers at this time to come out here," he cautioned.

The Reverend David Zeisberger was in charge at Lichtenau, a Moravian mission about two miles from Goschachking. He and White Eyes were on friendly terms, and it's likely that the chief, who couldn't read or write in

English, had dictated to Zeisberger the letter addressed to Colonel Morgan. As it happened, Zeisberger also wrote to Morgan on the 19th from Goschachking.

"White Eyes and I are blamed and accused before the governor at Detroit for giving you intelligence of the affairs in the Indian Country," Zeisberger said. He explained that the chief was measured in his remarks to Morgan. "I can tell you that he wisheth an army might come out now—the sooner the better, for its high time. All thoughts of bringing about a peace with the (Indian) nations, especially with the Wyandots, are in vain," Zeisberger said. ". . . White Eyes thinks that the only help you can afford him is to send an army against the Wyandots, etcetera."

The missionary then proceeded to provide military intelligence to the colonel: "A party of 80 Wyandots, mostly from over the Lake (Erie), are gone to Weelunk (Wheeling,

*The illustration is based on an 1862 oil painting by Christian Schussele titled The power of the Gospel: Zeisberger preaching to the Indians. Zeisberger was David Zeisberger, the Moravian missionary*

West Virginia) fort, as much as we know, and many other companies (of warriors) are gone to the settlements."

Apparently, the Moravians had not heard from Morgan in a long while. "We are afraid that your messengers may have had the misfortune to fall into the hands of some warriors if you have sent out any. That would make the matter worse if the letters should be intercepted and carried to Detroit," Zeisberger said.

In addition to hostile Indians, the Fort Pitt garrison had another major concern during the summer of 1778. Military forces throughout Pennsylvania were experiencing a severe shortage of lead. Essential for making bullets, the commodity had become so scarce that in April, Daniel Roberdeau, a member of the Continental Congress as well as a brigadier general in the Pennsylvania military, led militia troops up the Juniata River and took over production of ore at a lead mine in the Sinking Valley, north of present-day Hollidaysburg. He also built a smelter and began to ship lead ingots downriver.

Roberdeau's efforts helped ease the shortage, but military commanders at important posts still felt the pinch. As General Hand remarked sarcastically in a July 10 letter at Fort Pitt, "If there is not a possibility of obtaining lead, I wish we might be indulged with a cargo of bows and arrows, as our people are not yet expert enough at the sling to kill Indians with pebbles."

By September 1778, the 13 united colonies had become the 13 United States. U.S. officials summoned the Delawares to Fort Pitt for a treaty. They came. Messengers were also "sent to the Shawnees, inviting them to come to the treaty with the Delawares, but they declined," C. Hale

Sipe reported in his 1929 book, *The Indian Wars of Pennsylvania*. Sipe added that the only Shawnees who showed up belonged to "a small band under Nimwha, who lived with the Delawares at Coshocton."

The meeting lasted a week. "The interpreter was Job Chilloway, a Delaware from the Susquehanna, who had learned the English language from having lived for a number of years among the white people," Sipe said. It ended with the signing of a new treaty between the Delaware Nation and the United States on September 17.

The treaty began at Fort Pitt on September 12, a Saturday. White Eyes led the delegation of Delaware chiefs. Captain John Killbuck and Captain Pipe also had official roles. The two American commissioners, Andrew Lewis and Thomas Lewis, came from Virginia. General McIntosh attended, as did several top-level officers. These included Colonel Daniel Brodhead and Colonel John Gibson. Colonel Morgan, the Indian agent, had gone to Philadelphia and didn't attend.

In welcoming the Delawares, the commissioners remarked that "you alone of all the Western Indians seem inclined to hold fast the chain of friendship, and even in this instance it has contracted some rust of a very dangerous nature. The paths between us are grown up with bushes, so that they can scarce be seen. They are bloody."

The United States, the commissioners said, "sent us to offer you their friendship, if you accept the offer, they will consider you as their own people . . . In entering into engagements with the United States, nothing will be required of you but what will be for our mutual good and happiness."

If the commissioners led off with generalities, they soon brought up a specific issue: the Continental Army's need to cross Ohio to attack the British fort at Detroit, which was nearly 300 miles to the northwest. "General McIntosh who has the interest and good of your nation much at heart cannot reach your enemy otherwise than by marching his army through your country, to which . . . we presume you can have no objection," the commissioners said.

Two months earlier, Captain White Eyes wanted the Americans to send an army to the Tuscarawas immediately. That hadn't happened, but the Wyandots still menaced the Delawares, and White Eyes was pleased that McIntosh planned to march against Detroit. "I am greatly rejoiced to hear what you have now said," he said. "We shall consider well what you have said to us and return . . . an answer this afternoon, as we see you are desirous of proceeding on the intended expedition, which we hope will be the means of our living in peace."

On September 13, the second day of the treaty, White Eyes reported that the Delawares, as well as the Shawnee band headed by Chief Nimwha, willingly took hold of the Chain of Friendship. They were determined never to let go "though we should lose our lives."

White Eyes also expressed an eagerness to assist the Americans in clearing the path between the whites and the Delawares. He also voiced concern about the security of his tribe. "Brothers," he told the commissioners, "We now are become one people. The enemy Indians as soon as they hear it will strike us. We desire that our brethren will build some place for our old men, women and children to remain in safety, whilst our warriors go with you."

On the 14th, the commissioners read a draft of the treaty document to the Indians. Inclement weather on the 15th forced a postponement until the 16th. When the meeting resumed, White Eyes reported, "We have considered well everything mentioned in the Confederation. We like them well, and we are ready to join you in everything therein mentioned."

White Eyes promised that when the time came for McIntosh to leave Fort Pitt and move into Ohio, "as many of our warriors as can possibly be spared shall join you and go with you." He added, "We desire you not to think any of our people will have any objection to your marching through our country. On the contrary, they will rejoice to see you."

The treaty's sixth article warrants a mention, although nothing ever came of it. It stated that the United States guaranteed to the "Delawares, and their heirs, all their territorial rights in the fullest and most ample manner, as it hath been bounded by former treaties, as long as they the said Delaware nation shall abide by, and hold fast the chain of friendship now entered into."

Article 6 also stated that at some future time, the Delawares and "any other tribes who have been friends to the interest of the United States" could "form a state whereof the Delaware nation shall be the head, and have a representation in Congress."

Congress, of course, would have had to approve the formation of such a state. That never happened.

As the council concluded, the two U.S. commissioners, Andrew Lewis and Thomas Lewis, wrote their signatures on the document. In turn, the three Delaware chiefs—White Eyes, John Killbuck, and The Pipe—signed their marks.

As approved and signed by the Delaware chiefs as well as the U.S. commissioners, the treaty stated that the Indians "agree to give a free passage through their country to the troops . . . and . . . to conduct by the nearest and best ways to the posts, forts or towns of the enemies of the United States." The Delawares also pledged to provide the troops with "corn, meat, horses, or whatever may be in their power." The chiefs also agreed to have "the best and most expert warriors" join the U.S. troops as auxiliaries.

The records show that nearly a dozen military officers were present. They were: Brigadier General Lachlan McIntosh, commander of the Continental Army's Western Department; Colonel Daniel Brodhead of the Eighth Pennsylvania Regiment; Colonels William Crawford, John Campbell, and John Stephenson; Colonel John Gibson of the Thirteenth Virginia Regiment; Brigade Major A. Graham; Brigade Major Lachlan McIntosh, Jr.; Benjamin Mills; Captain Joseph L. Finley of the Eighth Pennsylvania Regiment; and Captain John Finley of the Eighth Pennsylvania Regiment.

Notably absent was Colonel Morgan, who had been the official Indian agent at Fort Pitt since 1776. Morgan had been in Philadelphia on business for several months.

# General McIntosh marches down the Ohio

General McIntosh needed horses, cattle, forage, and grain to reach Detroit. He also needed soldiers whose enlistments would allow them to serve for the duration of a lengthy campaign.

In August, as summer deepened, "General McIntosh has not above 200 effective men exclusive of militia who are stationed at small forts for ye protection of ye inhabitants," Commissioner Andrew Lewis reported.

Late summer and early autumn saw a troop buildup at Pittsburgh as regular soldiers belonging to the Continental Army and hundreds of militiamen arrived at Fort Pitt. McIntosh prepared to move out. It was late October when the general left Fort Pitt with about 1,300 men, most of them militia troops, and struck out for Fort Detroit, 300 miles to the northwest. White Eyes went along as a guide.

McIntosh led his army down the Ohio for about 30 miles. Around October 25, he stopped to erect a fort on Indian land on a bank overlooking the Ohio near the mouth of Beaver River. Constructing the post, which he called Fort McIntosh, took a full month.

The dullness of camp life becomes tiresome for the hundreds of soldiers not actively engaged in building the post. At least some men wandered into the nearby forest and amused themselves by carving their initials and names in the trunks of large trees. This was troublesome. The forest stood on land belonging to the Indians, and Indians knew that white people often marked large trees as the first step in claiming ownership of forest lands.

One of McIntosh's field officers, Colonel Daniel Brodhead, not only recognized the hazard these soldiers had created but also acted to minimize it. On October 22, he noted that general orders had already prohibited this practice. "Some persons yet unknown have presumed to mark trees in the woods with initial letters and their names at large," the colonel said. This gives "great uneasiness to our good friends and allies, the Delaware Nation," and needs to stop. He offered a reward of five pounds for soldiers who turned in violators.

McIntosh had another source of trouble: the troops showed little discipline with firearms. For instance, when a deer ran through the camp on October 26, a number of soldiers shot at it. The incident alarmed the general. He was disturbed that "the unmilitary practice of firing guns in and about camp (had) become so customary." Although he allowed some soldiers to go hunting, McIntosh forbid "shooting upon any other occasion." An order that he issued on October 27 said that "if two guns are heard within two or three minutes of each other by day, and one by night, that the drums shall beat to arms, and the whole line turn out immediately, prepared for action."

Located south of the Beaver's junction with the Ohio, the post occupied a strategic spot along the Great Path, a

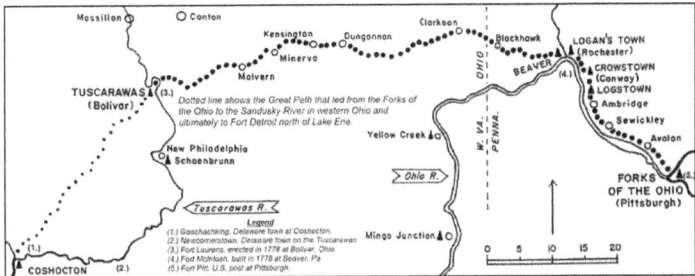

*Map of the Great Path.*

well-worn native trail that linked Fort Pitt and Fort Detroit. A second important trail, the Mahoning Path, left
the Great Path at this point and followed the Beaver north
to the native town of Kuskuskies before swinging to the
northwest. In *Indian Paths in Pennsylvania*, Wallace reports
that at present-day Akron, a branch of the Mahoning "ran
west to join the Great Path on the headwaters of the Sandusky River."

Boats coming down the Ohio or pack trains using the
Great Path could bring supplies from Pittsburgh to Fort
McIntosh. Wagons could also haul supplies overland along
a new road that McIntosh had soldiers build along the Vir-
ginia/Pennsylvania side of the river.

"This fort is built of well-hewn logs, with four bastions.
Its figure is an irregular square, the face to the river being
longer than the side to the land. It is about equal to a square
of 50 yards, is well built and strong against musketry; but
the opposite side of the river commands it entirely, and
a single piece of artillery from thence would reduce it."
So reported Arthur Lee, a U.S. Commissioner who came
to Fort McIntosh for an Indian treaty in December 1784.
Writing six years after the fort's construction, Lee left one

of the few descriptions of the defense.

Although General Mc-Intosh lauded the post as "a good strong fort," Colonel Brodhead faulted its location. "There is neither meadow, pasture, garden, or spring water convenient to that post."

Brodhead's criticisms had merit, especially the one about

*Colonel Daniel Brodhead*

water. Soldiers responsible for bringing water into the post had to descend the river bank and draw water directly from the Ohio. Decades later, John Cuppy, who had served in the Virginia Militia during the McIntosh campaign, recalled that to reach the river, the men used a specific path. Both sides of this path were lined by upright logs, called pickets, all the way down to the water, Cuppy said.

McIntosh found himself persistently vexed by the issue of adequate numbers of militia troops.

For starters, he had more soldiers from the regular army than Hand. In late spring, General Washington ordered two Continental Army regiments—the 13th Virginia and the 8th Pennsylvania—to leave eastern Pennsylvania for new postings at Pittsburgh. "These two regiments will march hence, with the full number of 250 men," Washington said, writing from Valley Forge in late May. He added that nearly 100 soldiers belonging to the 13th Virginia already were "now at and near Fort Pitt, and many deserters belonging to both (regiments) will come in when they find their regiments are to do duty" there.

McIntosh soon learned that the enlistments of most of the militia troops assigned to his expedition "will all expire the first day of January next." To remedy this, he used his authority as commander of the Western Department to order state militia officers in Pennsylvania and Virginia to call up more than 1,000 more troops. For example, in an October 30 letter to Colonel William Fleming of the Virginia Militia, McIntosh explained that militia commanders needed to "exert themselves in sending me a fresh supply of men soon to relieve those I have now."

Fleming was the county militia lieutenant in Virginia's Botetourt County. Politely but firmly, McIntosh told Fleming, "I must request of you now, Sir, to send me 200 active young men, properly officered, armed and accoutered as soon as possible, that I may not lose any posts or ground I may gain in the Indian Country."

The general told the colonel that the troops, preferably all enlisted to serve for six months, should reach Fort McIntosh as close to December 1 as possible. Their enlistments of "six months shall be from the time they arrive at my headquarters."

Within weeks, McIntosh learned that Virginia wasn't sending any replacements for the militia troops whose enlistments would expire at year-end. Indeed, Virginia didn't intend to send any troops at all that winter.

Earlier in the year, Governor Patrick Henry had enthusiastically supported McIntosh. He even told one militia commander, "I desire you will draw out so many men from the militia of your county as General McIntosh may demand."

It was then summer, and Henry had wanted quick compliance. "You are to take care, as the season is far advanced, that no time be lost to rendezvous the men according to the general's orders," the governor said in an August 6 letter. ". . . Every article of equipment which he calls for (should) be furnished in the most speedy and complete manner that circumstances will admit."

Even so, the governor saw the matter much differently by November 20. With winter approaching, Colonel Fleming should ignore the general's request for troops. "I am advised to countermand the general's orders, which I do hereby countermand," Henry said.

The Virginia Council had considered McIntosh's "demand for 200 men from each of the counties of Washington, Montgomery, Botetourt, Greenbrier and Rockbridge to join him on his expedition against the Indians, and that they are ordered to march immediately to the Delaware towns."

However, the Council concluded that "the impracticability of marching the troops at this inclement season through a country destitute of supplies; and that the want of tents, kettles, provisions, and indeed every necessary for such an undertaking, would inevitably render compliance with the general's request impossible."

Even as McIntosh prepared for an offensive campaign, he learned that nearly all of his militia troops would go home by New Year's Day.

McIntosh also saw many other things also go wrong. His officers began experiencing significant difficulties in obtaining supplies, especially forage for the horses and cattle. Horses were in short supply, even though hundreds would be needed to haul supplies and equipment as the army moved away from the Ohio and headed toward the

inland Delaware towns along the Tuscarawas and Muskingum rivers.

The general's plan called for drovers to herd cattle to
Fort McIntosh for slaughtering. The beef would be pro-
cessed and salted, then shipped with the army on pack-
horses. But when a herd of cattle arrived at Fort McIntosh
on November 3, the animals proved to be in "extremely
poor" condition. As the general reported afterward, the
animals had been exhausted by a trek of "400 or 500 miles"
from the settlements east of the Alleghenies. That's not all.
The soldiers at Fort McIntosh "could not slaughter them
for want of salt."

To remedy this, McIntosh, on November 5, told his
quartermasters to immediately send 500 horses "to Fort
Cumberland to bring flour and salt" to Fort McIntosh.
Located along the Potomac River, Fort Cumberland was
more than 100 miles to the southeast. The road that linked
the two forts crossed mountainous terrain.

The general also wanted an additional 300 horses
brought to Fort McIntosh, provided they were "fit for service," so they could haul "forage that is purchased on this
side of the Allegheny Mountains."

The army's quartermasters found it nearly impossible
to buy forage from the western farmers. To counter this,
McIntosh, on October 19, ordered Colonel Archibald
Steel, a deputy quartermaster-general in the Continental
Army at Fort Pitt, to take what he needed.

"Impress without any delay any quantity of grain not
exceeding 50,000 bushels, and any quantity of hay that
you will find necessary," the general said. In executing the
order, the soldiers were to use "as little violence as possible."

McIntosh explained that "every other means has failed in obtaining any forage for the expedition." Although the campaign against Detroit would bring about "their own salvation and future security from the savages and other enemies," the growers were "demanding more than double the price" that they "got last summer."

To the general's chagrin, the farmers were more willing to sell their grain to whiskey distillers—"whom this side of the mountains is overrun with" and willing to pay "any price."

All these complications delayed McIntosh's departure for Fort Detroit, which stood 300 miles northwest of Fort Pitt. Without allowing for inclement weather, an army moving at the average rate of 10 miles a day could conceivably march to Fort Detroit in a month, but by early November, McIntosh had gone only a tenth of the distance. Accustomed to the milder winters of Georgia, he may not have appreciated the severity of Ohio Valley winters or known that some years they came early.

# The 18th-century cold case of Colonel White Eyes

Better known a mong 18th-century whites as White Eyes, the Delaware chief Coquetageghton entered the written record in June 1762. He was among a number of Indians that the Moravian missionary Christian Frederick Post escorted that year from the native towns in eastern Ohio for a treaty with the governor of Pennsylvania in Lancaster

At the time, White Eyes lived in a log cabin at the mouth of the Beaver River, some 30 miles below Pittsburgh. The Indians called the place "sakunk," which means "the mouth of a stream."

Post remarked in his journal that "White Eye [*sic*] is one of the cleverest Indians" he had met. The missionary was more than qualified to make this observation. He had lived with native peoples in New York, Connecticut, and Ohio; spoke their languages; married an Indian woman; and occasionally served as a frontier diplomat.

White Eyes' cabin stood along the Great Path, a well-used Native American trail that led from The Forks of the Ohio to the Tuscarawas settlements. The trail was so narrow that travelers had to go in single-file. Post said White Eyes "liveth alone to oblige those who passeth by."

The previous September, a Pennsylvania trader named James Kenny had traveled down the Ohio in a flat-bottom boat. Responsible for the trading post at Fort Pitt, Kenny said that when he and his party reached the Beaver, they pulled their bateaux ashore at the home of "Gray Eyes or Sir William Johnson so called, one of ye heads of ye Delawares."

The chief—who later became better known as White Eyes—wasn't there. "He was gone to ye treaty now held at Detroit, some women and children being at home," Kenny wrote in his journal. "He has a good shingled house and several stables and cow houses under one roof."

British soldiers had built the structures in the years following the fall of Fort Duquesne in 1758.

The chief's family apparently made the travelers feel welcome because "we pitched our tent near ye house and made us a fire," Kenny said.

Two native men "about dusk came in from hunting. They sat with us some time, and we gave each some bread and a dram," Kenny said. One was named Turnum, and he "talks English well and being observing ye stars he could show us ye North Star and ye Great Bear and says ye Indians knows them and ye planets by particular names very well and observes their motions . . ."

Around 1770, White Eyes moved 100 miles to the southwest. David Jones, a missionary from New Jersey who traveled through the Ohio Country, found him living along the Tuscarawas not far from Newcomer's Town. In his journal entry for February 12, 1773, Jones noted that he and his companions were traveling along the Tuscarawas, headed for Newcomerstown. At one point, "we crossed the river in a canoe, our horses swimming by its side," Jones wrote. "The country began to be hilly, interspersed with some barren plains. We passed Captain White Eye's Town, but this noted Indian was down Ohio, . . . so that I could not have the satisfaction of seeing him this time."

The missionary noted that "I saw him several times the first visit (in 1772). He was the only Indian I met with in all my travels that seemed to have a design of accomplishing something future. He told me that he intended to be religious, and have his children educated. He saw that their way of living would not answer much longer—game grew scarce—they could not much longer pretend to live by hunting, but must farm, etc."

During the 1760s and 1770s, White Eyes exerted considerable influence on events in Ohio and at Fort Pitt. He frequently attended treaties, sometimes at Fort Pitt and other times at Fort Detroit. He had a well-deserved reputation for being outspoken. When acting as a tribal spokesman in formal meetings, White Eyes sometimes made comments that exceeded the remarks he had been instructed to make. For instance, historian Paul Wallace writes that "his appeals to the Continental Congress in 1776 brought him a rebuke from Netawatwees for going beyond what had been authorized by the Delaware council."

John Heckewelder not only knew White Eyes during this period, but his writing also suggests that he admired the man and, more than that, regarded him as a friend. In the missionary's pages, the Delaware leader comes across as a smart and spirited individual who acted boldly to influence events.

For instance, in October and November of 1775, White Eyes took part in a treaty that commissioners sent by the 2nd Continental Congress held at Pittsburgh. None of the Moravian missionaries from Ohio were present, but Delaware chiefs who attended subsequently told them what had happened. Years later, in writing his *Narrative of the Mission of the United Brethren Among the Delaware and Mohegan Indians*, Heckewelder reconstructed comments that White Eyes made after a speaker for the Seneca Nation chastised him "in a haughty tone" for openly expressing support for the rebellious American colonies.

"White Eyes," the Moravian wrote, ". . . with his usual spirit and an air of disdain, rose and replied that he well knew that the Six Nations considered his nation as a conquered people . . . You say . . . that you had conquered me, that you had cut off my legs, had put a petticoat on me, giving me a hoe and corn pounder in my hands, saying, 'Now, woman, your business henceforward shall be to plant and hoe corn, and pound the same for bread, for us men and warriors!'"

The Delaware didn't dispute this, but he urged the Seneca and his companions to "look . . . at my legs! If, as you say, you had cut them off, they have grown again to their proper size! The petticoat I have thrown away, and have put on my proper dress! The corn hoe and pounder I have exchanged for these firearms, and I declare that l am a man!"

All the Indians attending the conference knew that the Six Nations claimed ownership of the country to the west of the Ohio and Allegheny Rivers, but White Eyes challenged this notion. "Waving his hand in the direction of the Allegheny River, he exclaimed, 'and all the country on the other side of that river is mine,' " Heckewelder reported. His listeners understood that by "mine," the chief meant "my tribe's."

In February 1778, news reached the Delaware settlements along the Muskingum and Tuscarawas rivers that the British "governor of Detroit was determined to compel all the Indians . . . to turn out and fight the American people, or rebels, as he termed them," Heckewelder reported. "He would even punish all such as did not obey his orders." False rumors often swept through Ohio, but in this case, the news arrived at Goschachking in writing. The Moravian missionaries at nearby Lichtenau "were sorry to see by a letter, which bore the signature of the governor, that . . . what they had heard on the subject proved to be true," Heckewelder said.

On top of that, three men who had defected from the Americans and become notorious Tories—Heckewelder

*Lichtenau monument. (Photo by Robert B. Swift.)*

described them as "very suspicious and dangerous characters"—arrived in Goschachking. They were Alexander McKee, Matthew Elliot, and Simon Girty. They spread "abominable falsehoods respecting the war" and warned the Indians that the Americans planned "to kill and destroy the whole Indian race, be they friends or foes, and possess themselves of their country."

This report caused "consternation," with many Delawares deciding to abandon their neutrality and go over to the British immediately. Calling a council, White Eyes persuaded the warriors to delay for "10 days, during which time they might obtain more certain information as to the truth of the assertions of these men."

The chief told the warriors "that if they meant in earnest to go out, they should not go without him. He had taken peace measures, in order to save the nation from utter destruction. But . . . if they had determined to . . . go out against the Americans, he would go out with them."

White Eyes said he didn't intend to be "like the bear hunter, who sets the dogs on the animal to be beaten about with his paws, while he keeps at a safe distance. No! He would himself lead them on, place himself in the front, and be the first who should fall. They only had to determine on what they meant to do, for his own mind was fully made up not to survive his nation."

The warriors agreed to wait.

Heckewelder had been away from Ohio for many months. By coincidence, he returned to the Tuscarawas on the eighth day of the 10-day grace period. When he reached Goschachking in the late morning of the 10th day, many Indians turned out to see him. "But although I saluted them in passing them, not a single person returned the compliment, which . . . was no good omen."

The missionary was surprised when old friends and acquaintances gave him the cold shoulder. "Even Captain White Eyes and the other chiefs, who always had befriended me, now stepped back when I reached out my hand to them," Heckewelder said.

*John Heckewelder, missionary.*

The missionary asked why the Indians had become so unfriendly. White Eyes remarked that McKee, Elliot, and Girty had told the Delawares that "they no longer had a single friend among the American people."

Heckewelder replied, "Were I not their friend, they never would have seen me here."

White Eyes fired off a series of questions and demanded that Heckewelder answer each truthfully. The chief asked:

"Are the American armies all cut to pieces by the English troops?

"Is General Washington killed?

"Is there no more a Congress, and have the English hung some of them, and taken the remainder to England to hang them there?

"Is the whole country beyond the mountains in the possession of the English?

"Are the few thousand Americans who have escaped them, now embodying themselves on this side of the mountains for the purpose of killing all the Indians in this country, even our women and children?"

Up and down the street, people were paying close attention, and Heckewelder "declared before the whole assembly that not one word of what he (White Eyes) had just now told me was true."

At this point, Heckewelder told the people that General Hand, the commandant at Fort Pitt, had given him messages for White Eyes. Holding papers up for the Indians to see, the missionary said that these were speeches reassuring "the peaceable Delawares" at Goschachking that the Americans continued to be their friends.

Heckewelder recognized a man in the crowd, a drummer whose job it was to summon the villagers to important functions of the tribal council. "Accidentally catching the eye of the drummer, I called to him to beat the drum for the Assembly to meet for the purpose of hearing what their American brethren had to say to them."

In a loud voice, White Eyes asked the villagers if they wanted to hear what Heckewelder had to say. The crowd "as with one voice answered in the affirmative," Heckewelder said. "The drum was beat," and the villagers quickly moved "to the spacious council house. The speeches, all of which were of the most pacific nature, were read and interpreted to them."

At length, White Eyes stood up and spoke. He "took particular notice of the good disposition of the American people towards the Indians, observing that they had never as yet called on them to fight the English, knowing that wars were destructive to nations, that those had from the beginning of the war to the present time always advised them (the Indians) to remain quiet, and not take up the hatchet against either side," Heckewelder reported.

After this, the residents of Goschachking remained at peace with the Americans for the rest of White Eyes' life.

## How, where and when did White Eyes die?

For several years, White Eyes had been one of the strongest supporters of the American cause among the Ohio tribes. Suddenly, in late 1778, "he took the smallpox and died," Heckewelder reported.

This happened while White Eyes was "accompanying General McIntosh's army to Tuscarawas, where a fort was to be built for the protection of the peaceable Indians and frontier settlers." Heckewelder said.

One of the few military sources who mention White Eyes was Stephen Burkam, then a 16-year-old soldier in the Virginia Militia who took part in the McIntosh campaign. Interviewed by Dr. Lyman Draper more than 65 years later, an elderly Burkam said that General McIntosh brought White Eyes along as a guide. "White Eyes at Fort McIntosh was taken with the smallpox, and was sent to Pittsburg where he soon died," Burkam said. ". . . None others had small pox."

Draper reported the interview took place at Burkam's home near Wheeling, West Virginia, in 1845.

Curiously, news of White Eyes' death and the circumstances surrounding appears to be absent from the official correspondence of the principal military officers—notably General McIntosh and Colonels Brodhead and Gibson—who commanded American troops in the Western Department. Nor does the official correspondence of McIntosh's superior officer, General Washington, contain any references to the death of White Eyes. Two centuries later, these omissions appear as gaping holes in the official record. If smallpox killed the chief, why was there no official mention of it? If the chief fell victim to foul play, why didn't contemporary correspondence document it?

Months after McIntosh was reassigned to the war's eastern theater, Colonel Brodhead took over command of Fort Pitt and the western department. Scholars have located a letter in the colonel's letter book that was clearly intended to console White Eyes' family and friends following his death.

Writing to the Delawares on June 22, 1779, Brodhead described White Eyes as "an honest man and a great counsellor" and said, "it was the will of God to call him to himself last fall." Along with the letter, the colonel sent a belt of wampum intended for the chief's relatives, who "must be much troubled." The wampum was meant "to wipe off their tears and remove sorrow from your hearts." Without giving the location, Brodhead said, "I buried him in a fine place and put a shade over the grave to keep the rains, storms and sun off."

Brodhead didn't explain why the Continental Army waited more than seven months after White Eyes' death to offer condolences to his relatives formally. The chief's demise does, however, enter the official record in the days immediately following his death, albeit in a roundabout way. A document dated November 9, 1778, discloses that "the property of the late Colonel White Eyes of the Delaware Nation, deceased," was in Pittsburgh. Whatever the location and circumstances of the chief's death, Colonel

Archibald Steel ordered his personal belongings to be inventoried and cataloged. These items included:

A breechclout, or loincloth, fully trimmed;
A pair of scarlet breeches;
A pair of knee buckles;
A linen jacket;
A pair of old buckskin leggings;
Three pairs of shoes, one pair was new and the others were old;
A green coat faced with red with a patch;
A match coat;
A broach and earring;
A pair of spectacles;
A silver medal effigy of George the 3rd of Great Britain;
A beaver hat;
A knife case, and belt;
A rifle, pouch and horn; and
A pipe tomahawk.

Other personal possessions included:

A pair of saddle bags;
A large belt of wampum, 11 rows;
A quill-backed comb;
A pair of scissors;
A bundle of sundry papers; and
A small red pocket book with some papers and needles.

The report that smallpox killed White Eyes circulated throughout the frontier. Then, several years after the Revolution ended, George Morgan, the Indian agent at Fort Pitt in 1778, alleged that White Eyes "was treacherously put to death" while serving in the McIntosh campaign. In a letter written at Princeton, New Jersey, and dated May 18, 1784, Morgan asserted that he knew about the killing, but "I have never mentioned (it) to any one but Mr. (Charles) Thomson and two or three members of Congress." Addressed to an officer of the Continental Congress, the letter didn't disclose details of the murder. Thomson was secretary of Congress.

In 1776, Congress appointed Morgan as the Indian agent assigned to Fort Pitt. Morgan worked diligently to have the Delawares remain neutral. During the next several years, he and White Eyes developed a close working relationship. Morgan spent much of 1778 in Philadelphia and didn't return to Fort Pitt until January 2, 1779, nearly two months after White Eyes died. Consequently, Morgan had no first-hand information about the chief's death. He submitted his resignation to Congress in early May.

Morgan's allegations remained under wraps for nearly a century. An article by Isaac Craig that appeared in an 1883 issue of a periodical, *Historical Register: Notes and Queries, Historical and Genealogical,* quoted Morgan's letter and said it was only "recently brought to light."

Many 20th-century scholars accepted Morgan's allegation. As recently as 1972, historian C.A. Weslager reported in *The Delaware Indians* that White Eyes "was treacherously put to death, at the moment of his greatest exertions to serve the United States in whose service he held the commission of colonel."

In 1991, the late Earl P. Olmstead said, "White Eyes had been shot and killed by an American colonial militiaman." In his book, *Blackcoats among the Delaware, David Zeisberger on the Ohio Frontier,* Olmstead said that the National Archives has copies of Morgan's letters to federal officials, including the 1784 letter Olmstead said was addressed to Thomas Mifflin, then president of the Continental Congress. Olmstead noted the records exist on microfilm in the National Archives as part of the George Morgan Papers, 1776–1789. He said, "Copies of the manuscripts are in the author's files."

Morgan's 1784 letter raises many questions:

If a militia soldier did shoot White Eyes, why was the fact hushed up?

Where and when did the killing take place?

Was the soldier's identity known? Was he ever punished?

Was the story that White Eyes died of smallpox deliberately concocted as official disinformation? If so, who came up with it, and why?

Were military officials concerned with how the Delawares might react if they learned that White Eyes had been murdered?

Where was White Eyes buried? On what date did he die?

The soldiers and civilians at Fort Pitt knew that people could catch smallpox from blankets and clothing used by smallpox victims. Would the men who inventoried White Eyes's clothing at Pittsburgh have done so if the chief had died of smallpox?

Does the fact that the inventory was apparently conducted soon after his death, possibly within a matter of days, contradict or support the notion that smallpox killed him?

November 1778

# American troops go deeper into Ohio

By the end of October 1778, General McIntosh had become convinced that his plan to erect strong posts at strategic locations "as I go into the Indian Country . . . alarms the savages much."

"Several tribes have already applied to me for peace, but I have given them no encouragement yet," McIntosh said in an October 30 letter to an officer in the Virginia Militia.

Headed "to the Delaware towns . . . I propose setting off from here in two or three days, and build a fort there to secure these people in our interest." Despite the lateness of the season, once his soldiers had constructed the new fort, "I may make excursions to some of the hostile towns."

Fort McIntosh was nearly finished when, on November 4, General McIntosh finally marched west with 1,000 men, following the trail that linked Fort Pitt on the east and Fort Detroit in the northwest. It may have been around this time that White Eyes died.

General McIntosh decided to build another fort where the path crossed the Tuscarawas River at present-day Bolivar, Ohio. The choice was highly strategic. As General Henry Clinton, the British commander at New York, said months later, it was "on the direct road to Detroit."

The construction site was about 75 miles from Fort McIntosh, and McIntosh had thought it would only take several days to reach the location. He hadn't anticipated that the supply train would slow his advance considerably. "This is the 10th day I have been upon my march," McIntosh said in a November 13 letter to Lieutenant Colonel Richard Campbell, who had remained behind at Fort McIntosh. "I am not 50 miles from your fort."

The general blamed the lack of progress on the packhorses. Their poor condition was "scandalous," he declared. The army's quartermasters had provided the animals. "Above one half of them tires every day before we travel two or three miles, and the woods is strewed with those that have given out and died."

By mid-November, his detachment still needed to march another "16 or 17 miles to Tuscarawas." McIntosh said, "I much fear I shall not be able to carry our provisions and stores that length."

Back at Fort McIntosh, Colonel Campbell was having troubles of his own. The shortage of fodder had become so severe that the horses were starving. "My wagon horses are dropping down in the gears for want of forage," the colonel told the general. By gears, Campbell meant the front wheels and axle of a wagon.

Nonetheless, the colonel said he hoped, "I shall be able to have a thousand bushels here in a few days from this time." He reported that he planned to use the Ohio River rather than the road along it to accomplish this, and that he had "ordered one of my officers and 20 men and all the boats up the river to bring forage from where it can be had."

Campbell had other concerns as well. McIntosh had marched off without completing work on Fort McIntosh and left specific instructions: "You are to get the fort finished as soon as possible . . . the gates are to be hung and secured . . . and the bastions put in a proper state of defense . . . with the tower in the front. The barracks may be finished the last."

The Delawares wanted McIntosh to construct the fort on the Tuscarawas along a well-used trail to protect them against pro-British Indians who lived west of the Delaware villages. But the Americans also planned to use the fort to stage an assault against Fort Detroit. McIntosh made this clear in a letter to Chief Killbuck months later. "You gave us leave yourselves . . . to make forts for our provision upon your land on our path to Detroit," he said.

Known as the Great Path, this well-used thoroughfare connected the Forks of the Ohio on the east with Fort Detroit in the northwest. From Pittsburgh, this trail followed the Ohio River for a little more than 25 miles before swinging inland at the mouth of the Beaver River, near the site of Fort McIntosh, and heading west toward the Tuscarawas and the Sandusky Rivers. The British post, situated north of Lake Erie's western end, stood along the Detroit River, which carried water from Lake Huron south to Lake Erie.

Also on November 13, messengers sent by the Delaware chiefs arrived in General McIntosh's camp with news that their warriors would join the expedition in a few days, either "at or perhaps this side (of) the Tuscarawas." To help his men recognize the Delawares, the general gave the messengers "a white flag with 14 red stripes."

With his native allies in camp, McIntosh ordered his soldiers to be especially cautious. His orders for the day stated that "no parties are to go any distance ahead of the army" and that "every person is to be exceedingly cautious to distinguish well whether any Indians they meet are friends or enemies before they fire upon them."

The men were also forbidden to sell merchandise to the natives or trade with them.

Over the next several days, as the column moved deeper into Indian Country, McIntosh issued a spate of orders to keep his men safe.

On Nov. 16, for example, the general said that "all the officers and soldiers are desired to collect and save all the deer tails they can get and wear them in their hats." He wanted "our friend Indians to do the same . . ." Doing this would help to "distinguish ourselves . . . from our enemies," he said.

Ever since leaving Fort Pitt weeks earlier, many soldiers had taken to firing their weapons, seemingly, whenever they felt like it. As early as September 30, Colonel Daniel Brodhead had issued a formal order forbidding troops in the 8th Pennsylvania from discharging their weapons without authorization. This practice resulted in the " very extraordinary waste of the best ammunition belonging to the regiment," Brodhead said. To enforce the ban, he instructed the officers to "immediately mark the powder-horns and count the bullets of each rifleman in the regiment, and count the cartridges of (each) musketeer."

But the troops persisted in firing their weapons as the army moved deeper into Indian Country. On November 17, now that "some enemy Indians have been seen near our camp," the unauthorized discharge of firearms must stop, McIntosh said. "The repeated orders issued against firing guns wantonly is so shamefully neglected, any soldier who detects another shooting a gun hereafter without leave, shall, upon conviction of the offender, be entitled to a month's pay extra." Violators would face a court martial.

McIntosh feared that his officers had become so accustomed to soldiers shooting their weapons for amusement that they might not respond to the sound of guns being fired during an attack. "If any officer commanding a party next (to) where a shot is heard does not immediately rush to the place . . . to see if it is an enemy, he shall be put under an arrest for breach of orders."

By November 21, McIntosh had reached the Tuscarawas and set up his headquarters on the river's west bank. Wintry weather had already set in. The soldiers quickly began felling trees in the nearby woods and cutting them into 18-foot lengths for use as pickets in the fort's stockade.

Decades later, one veteran—Virginia militiaman John Cuppy—remembered that the soldiers built the post, which McIntosh called Fort Laurens, on a high bank with no timber. The location had been "barren back for half a mile or more, and the men had to carry in the timber, four or five to a stick," Cuppy said. The fort's palisades were "made mostly of large, hard-wood timber, split, some six inches thick, bullet-proof, planted in trenches three feet deep, solidly packed around, and extending 15 feet above ground."

The soldiers lived in the clearing. "The army encamped in the open ground in a semi-circle around Fort Laurens, some distance from the fort, but not so far back as the woods," said Cuppy, then 17. "Every mess, composed of six or seven men, had a tent."

Around this time, General McIntosh made an important decision that affected every soldier. With "our supplies uncertain," he curtailed rations "to one pound of flour per man until a supply arrives." To compensate, "each man is to be served with one pound and a half of beef per day, which the commissaries will strictly observe till further orders."

McIntosh soon abandoned any thoughts about marching against Fort Detroit by year-end. As recently as September, the general had hoped to do this, but November turned cold as his troops erected the walls and barracks at Fort Laurens, and McIntosh doubted "whether we can do anything against the enemy this season."

Life at Fort Laurens soon became unpleasant. As elderly veterans, John Cuppy and his comrades remembered that food supplies began to run out before the fort was finished. A herd of cattle had accompanied the soldiers on the march from Fort McIntosh to provide fresh meat, but the animals had had little to eat, either along the trail through the woods or at the site of the new post. "The beeves got very poor towards the close of November and early December," Cuppy said.

Another veteran, Stephen Burkam, recalled that "provisions began to fail" soon after the army reached the Tuscarawas, and that the troops were "put on short allowance, (a) quarter of a pound of flour each p(er) day."

A third man, Jacob White, reported that while Fort Laurens was under construction, "a party of 40 or 50 Indians, including some squaws and children, made their appearance with a white flag, and begged peace. General

McIntosh held a conference with them, and they retired friendly."

White, a 19-year-old militiaman, living along the Monongahela south of Pittsburgh, didn't say whether Indians brought food for the soldiers, but Cuppy said they had. He said the natives "frequently visited the camp, and brought fine fat haunches of venison, bear meat and turkeys," which they "presented to the officers, who gave them . . . fire-water in return."

Cuppy emphasized that the Native American who came into camp "were entirely peaceable." He said he didn't recall any "attacks from them during the expedition." On the contrary, "the Indians, both men and women would have frequent dances, a hundred or more together, the taller taking the lead, and others falling into the circle, according to their height, the shortest bringing up the rear, and dancing around in the circle, to the rude music derived from beating upon a kettle by an old Indian, intermingled with occasional yells."

Fort Laurens took shape as the weeks passed. Lacking a spring within its walls, the post "relied upon the river for (a) supply of water," Cuppy said. White recalled that the post occupied high ground on the river's west bank. "The fort was built on an eminence, at the foot of which, some 40 or 50 feet from the fort, several fine springs burst forth . . . Between the bank and the river was a narrow bottom," White said. "This was the highest spot of ground in that region."

According to John Cuppy, "The gate was on the west side of the fort. There was one blockhouse, about 20 feet square, which was directly to the right of the gate, and next to it." Its outside wall formed part of the fort's stockade wall. "About six feet above the ground, the block-house was made a foot wider on the wall side, and made to over-jut, so if Indians came up, the garrison could shoot down through this open jut directly upon an enemy below," Cuppy said.

The elderly veteran recalled that there were "portholes all around about five feet from the floor, and some two or three feet apart, . . . for the garrison to fire (through) in case of an attack, with a rude roof slanting one way, and that within the fort."

The longer that construction went on, the shorter provisions became. Concern grew about how the army could stretch its food supply to feed 1,000 men. By late November, McIntosh came upon a partial solution. One officer, Captain Basil Prather, had been able to "put a stop to the unmilitary practice of wasting ammunition and firing guns wantonly." The general decided "to send four men from each regiment every day to hunt deer for the benefit of their respective corps." He assigned Prather to take charge of the daily hunts.

Around this time, the general decided to postpone any attack on Detroit until spring and to have most of the soldiers return to Fort McIntosh.

By December 2, the soldiers had begun constructing two rows of cabins inside Fort Laurens. McIntosh offered the men an incentive to complete them within a week. Also, his original plan had called for building "four good blockhouses" along the trail back to Fort McIntosh, but he was now willing to reduce the number. "The general promises and assures the militia that if they exert themselves and will finish the two side rows of cabins laid out for them by

Monday (December 7) night with what they have already begun, they shall have but one blockhouse to raise upon the road to Fort McIntosh."

General McIntosh had a variety of issues to resolve before setting out for Fort McIntosh. One involved courts martial for soldiers who had had commercial dealings with the Indians. The records show: "Captain Isaac Pierce . . . was tried for dealing with Indians contrary to a positive order, to which Captain Pierce pleads guilty, and confesses he did give an Indian a shirt and two dollars for two deerskins." The court sentenced Pierce to acknowledge his guilt and to receive a reprimand, but McIntosh thought this punishment was too lenient, and "continues Captain Pierce under arrest."

A second officer, "Sergeant John Aspy of the Light Dragoons, was tried for the same crime . . . and confessed he gave an Indian the buttons of his coat for two fawn skins. The court sentenced him to be reduced to a private sentinel and receive 20 lashes on his bare back." Aspy subsequently suffered the reduction in rank but didn't receive the whipping.

As he prepared to return to Fort McIntosh, the general placed Colonel Gibson in command at Fort Laurens with a garrison representing only part of Gibson's regiment. A return of troops dated December 21, 1778, showed the post with a total of 181, including 172 soldiers belonging to the two Continental regiments and five women.

On December 5, McIntosh ordered a treat: "All officers and soldiers in the line are to be served with a gill of whiskey each, and the general is sorry horses could not be procured to bring more of that necessary article." A gill was equal to four fluid ounces. Not all soldiers were to be served. "Those who came up with the whiskey are not to have any as two kegs are missing," the general said.

McIntosh left a small quantity of liquor behind, but this wasn't intended for Gibson or his garrison. According to McIntosh's general order of December 8, there were "two kegs of the whiskey that is for the use of the Indians, to be left with Colonel Gibson." All other whiskey was "to be distributed throughout the line."

As he had done when leaving Fort McIntosh six weeks earlier, McIntosh marched off without finishing the new fort. Before he left, the general made Gibson responsible for completing its construction.

Adverse weather conditions became a factor in preventing the soldiers from installing posts in the stockade speedily. As Gibson explained in a December 21 letter, "I have almost (finished the) setting up and ramming the pickets." The work might have been performed faster, but ". . . the distressed situation of the men for clothing prevents the work from going on so briskly as otherwise it would."

McIntosh left Fort Laurens around December 9. Veteran John Cuppy recalled that "snow had fallen before they left the Tuscarawas." He described walking over "ground covered with some half a dozen inches of snow while marching from the Tuscarawas to Fort McIntosh."

Cuppy characterized the return march as proceeding "not in much order, except each company kept together, and all were scattered along, perhaps over half the whole distance." Veteran Jesse Ellis recalled that the men didn't encounter any Indians.

General McIntosh had distributed little food to the men headed back to Fort McIntosh. "The scanty allowance of beef was very poor," said Cuppy, who added, "the troops generally suffered for want of food."

Provisions were soon exhausted, and "the main army . . . marched on return without a particle of anything" to eat, Stephen Burkam said. He, Cuppy, and Ellis all said that many men forced themselves to eat an unlikely material— leather chips cut from the hides of cows slaughtered for beef along the trail in November and served to the troops as they had marched out to Fort Laurens. These hides had been discarded along the trail.

On the return trip, the troops were so hungry that, according to Ellis, the soldiers cut up and roasted 36 of these old, dried hides in just one night. As Cuppy remarked, "Some of the soldiers were glad to make use of the hides of the beeves that had been killed on the outward march, and crisp them over the fire, and eat them as they could."

Occasionally, "some of the militia would venture out and kill deer," Ellis said.

Cuppy recalled that some of the men in his mess had pulled guard duty the night before they left Fort Laurens. They had somehow managed "to secure a small sack of flour, which they carried some distance into the woods and baked up, throwing away the bag, and dividing the bread."

The veteran said he came along the trail and "met one poor young fellow named John Bell, sitting by the roadside crying, saying he was so weak he could not proceed any further." Cuppy said that he shared his bread with Bell "and encouraged him to renew the march, which he did."

By December 13, the soldiers had reached Fort McIntosh. In general orders issued on that date, "the general congratulates the troops upon their return to this post on their way home after establishing two important posts in the enemy's country."

McIntosh used the occasion to express his "hearty thanks" to the Virginia militia troops "for a conduct during this campaign which would do honor to the best regular troops." Not all soldiers received the general's salutations. Without mentioning names, he said there were "a few individuals who he hopes will stay at home the next time, and never come here again to poison and corrupt an army so determined to serve their country."

Back at Fort Pitt by December 29, McIntosh reported to Pennsylvania authorities two positive accomplishments:

First, "I erected a good strong fort for the reception and security of prisoners and stores, upon the Indian side of Ohio below Beaver Creek, with barracks for a regiment." This was Fort McIntosh.

Second, he erected another post "about 100 miles west of this place." This was Fort Laurens, "which I expect will keep the savages in awe, and secure the peace of the frontiers effectually in this quarter hereafter if they are well supported."

Fort Laurens, he asserted, would "also facilitate any future enterprises that may be attempted that way."

# Enemy warriors besiege Fort Laurens

Indians allied with the English saw immediately that the erection of Fort Laurens posed a threat against Fort Detroit. They realized that to reach the British post, McIntosh would march a combined force of Continental soldiers and militia from Virginia and Pennsylvania, quite possibly augmented by Delaware warriors, through their own villages along the Sandusky River in western Ohio.

In late December 1778, Pomoacan, the Wyandot half-king, warned Chief Killbuck and, through him, the Americans at Fort Laurens, Fort McIntosh, and Fort Pitt: "If you are determined to proceed on your road to Detroit, I desire you will keep at some distance from my towns, then I shall be able to prevent my foolish young men from doing any harm."

"Should you march through my towns," Pomoacan cautioned, the young Wyandot warriors would likely become so incensed that "probably I could not be able to" restrain them. Killbuck apparently dictated the Wyandot's warning to Colonel John Gibson, the commandant at Fort Laurens. A century ago, historians who compiled a large collection of Revolutionary War documents said the letter containing Pomoacan's warning was in Gibson's handwriting.

By late December, provisions were running very low at Fort Laurens. Colonel Gibson planned to send Samuel Semple, a Pittsburgh innkeeper who had come on the Fort Laurens campaign as a deputy quartermaster general, to Goschachking, a Delaware town about 50 miles farther west. Indians there had indicated a willingness to sell food supplies to the army. "With what cattle he can purchase, I am in hopes we shall have beef enough, and that we shall also have a sufficient quantity of flour until a farther supply can be sent," the colonel said.

As Gibson advised General McIntosh in a December 21 letter, Captain Killbuck and seven other Delawares had stopped at the new fort. "I intend sending Mr. Semple with him to Goschachking with about 20 horses to purchase cattle, corn, etc. . . . As he (Killbuck) has promised to conduct him back, I am in hopes there will be no danger."

Eleven days later, Gibson reported to McIntosh, "Mr. Semple . . . is not yet returned. The weather has been very cold and the rivers very high, which I imagine may have detained him."

At some point after January 1, Semple returned from Goschachking with provisions, but whatever food he brought was soon consumed because the quartermaster started on a second trip to the Delaware town in mid-January.

Despite Heckewelder's description of Goschachking (present-day Coshocton, Ohio, where the Tuscarawas joins the Muskingum) as the headquarters of the Delaware Nation's peace chiefs, the town proved an unsafe place for Semple during his second visit. He had "pitched his tent opposite to the village, leaving one of his men to take care of the camp and horses," according to Heckewelder. Semple "had scarcely crossed the Muskingum River, which lay between his camp and the town, when the scalp yell was heard in the direction of his camp. The people of the town running to the bank, just saw the murderers go off in triumph with the scalp of the man and the horses."

Colonel Gibson later identified the dead man as John Nash, a Continental soldier belonging to the 13th Virginia Regiment. The killing happened on the afternoon of January 23, the day after Semple had arrived. The next afternoon, "two Delawares shot three of the best horses and carried off two more, 10 bags, some bells, two saddles and some blankets," Gibson reported.

A related shooting occurred toward the end of January. Two other soldiers belonging to the 13th Virginia were returning to Goschachking from Lichtenau, a nearby Moravian mission. One of the Delawares who had robbed Semple's camp the previous week "hid himself on the road from the Moravian town," Gibson reported. When the soldiers came along, "he fired on them." He wounded a soldier named Peter Parchment, who managed to run a few yards after dropping his firearm. "The Indian took up the gun and was going to fire again, but was prevented by Captain Johnny, (a Delaware chief) who happened to be coming along the road, who hallooed to him not to shoot," Gibson said.

The assailant "then ran off and crossed the river" to escape.

As for the wounded soldier, "the ball broke Parchment's arm (and) entered his breast, but has since been taken out," Gibson reported.

Semple and his escort returned to Fort Laurens on January 31. Along with "corn and skins" purchased from the Delawares, the quartermaster also brought an ominous message from Chief Killbuck. In talking to Semple on January 29, the chief acknowledged how dangerous the country had become for the Americans. "I shall take all the care I can of Mr. Semple and his men." the chief said. He promised "to deliver him safe unto you again. I send 20 of my men with them. Nobody shall be able to hurt them."

The chief also said he had "ordered three of my men to stay with you" at Fort Laurens. "They are to be with you as guards for 15 days."

The message included a warning. "I have heard that all nations are gathering to attack the fort at Tuscarawas at the full of this moon," Killbuck said. "I assure you I shall be very watchful." The next full moon was only a few days away.

Mid-winter events more than warranted Killbuck's precautions. The British at Fort Detroit and the pro-British Native Americans living along the Sandusky River in west-central Ohio had decided to destroy Fort Laurens.

In late January, news arrived at Lichtenau that missionary David Zeisberger said was "not favorable at all if true." Native informants had told Zeisberger "that the warriors of the nations were gathering together at Sandusky and Detroit" and that on "the full moon after this next they would in a large body attack Fort Laurens and cut off all communication."

In 1779, the first full moon after January 20 occurred on February 1; The next one was on March 2.

Were the British to capture Fort Laurens, "the Delawares who at present are very few in number would be forced to join the enemies," the missionary said.

Also in late January, the army at Fort McIntosh encountered difficulty in supplying Fort Laurens. "A small party of Mingos" waylaid a detachment of 16 soldiers along the trail linking forts Laurens

*David Zeisberger, missionary.*

and McIntosh, which were some 75 miles apart. Commanded by Captain John Clark, men belonging to the 8th Pennsylvania had escorted a shipment of supplies to Fort Laurens from Fort McIntosh. Headed back to McIntosh, they had gone about three miles when the Indians ambushed them. General McIntosh reported that the hostiles killed two soldiers and captured a third, along "with his saddle bags and all his letters." Clark and the other 12 men hurried back to Fort Laurens without further incident.

By coincidence, Delaware messengers from Goschachking were in the Wyandot towns along the Sandusky River when warriors arrived "with a prisoner and two scalps and a great many letters" taken in the ambush, Killbuck later told Colonel Gibson. The letters apparently included some with information that the Delaware chiefs had sent to the American officers at Fort Pitt and Fort McIntosh.

The content of the letters angered the Wyandot half-king, Pomoacan, who told the Delawares, "I have told you

*David Zeisberger's grave. (Photo by Robert B. Swift.)*

a year ago (to) leave off sending letters" to the Americans. He had ordered the Delawares to "quit them entirely."

Pomoacan, who spoke bluntly, had referred to the Americans as Virginians. Killbuck's messengers subsequently gave the Goschachking chief and counselors an unadorned rendition of his words: "I am quite astonished at you and your works, and must needs think you are the cause of the Virginians building a fort at Tuscarawas, I cannot think otherwise but you have sold them that land entirely. I now tell you again, Cousin at Goschachking, do not go any more to the Virginians . . . for if I see you there, I will consider you as a Virginian, and kill you the same as I will kill the Virginians."

If Zeisberger had a reason for concern, the British did not, at least not in the immediate future. "The Indian Expedition against Detroit under the command of General McIntosh . . . is at present entirely at an end," General Henry Clinton, the British commander-in-chief, reported from New York on February 1.

Writing to General Frederick Haldimand in Canada, Clinton indicated that at least as long as the winter lasted, Fort Detroit had little to fear from McIntosh's troops. He noted that "1,500 of them marched in October from Fort Pitt; (and) stopped at a place . . . about 150 miles from Fort Pitt, where they began to build a temporary fort." Sickness, combined with "their difficulty . . . in procuring provisions," had prompted McIntosh to return to the Ohio River. "Nothing in that department can be done till next April or May," Clinton said.

With White Eyes dead, the Delawares no longer wanted their warriors to participate in McIntosh's march against Detroit. Reporting to McIntosh from Fort Laurens in mid-February, Colonel Gibson also disclosed that Killbuck had begun to back away from the Delawares' pledge, made at Fort Pitt in September, to send warriors to fight alongside the Americans in the assault on the British post.

Not quite three months had passed since White Eyes died. In a February 13 letter to McIntosh, the colonel reported that Killbuck "says that Colonel White Eyes and I deceived them—that the tomahawk was forced on them . . . that it was never meant by them to join us as warriors, that they were only to pilot us." In other words, the chiefs had agreed to guide McIntosh across Ohio but hadn't consented for their warriors to fight against the British soldiers and their Indian allies.

In a related development, rumors persisted that pro-British warriors were about to attack Fort Laurens. On February 18, Killbuck sent word to General McIntosh that an Indian who had visited a Delaware town on the Upper Miami River in western Ohio arrived in Goschachking with troubling news.

"The commandant at Detroit," Killbuck said, "had told the Indians to make an attempt on Fort Laurens, and in case they were not able to take it he would come himself and help them . . . that the warriors would come to Goschachking for provision and if we should not give it them freely, they would take by force what they pleased and kill us. Likewise, if they met anybody at some distance from our towns, they would kill him. If they should meet any Delaware Indians at Fort Laurens, they should be treated as prisoners and be killed."

These warriors, Killbuck said, wanted to capture Fort Laurens because the Americans had "some ammunition in the fort which they wanted . . ." After capturing Fort Laurens, "they would only cast a few bullets and then proceed to Fort McIntosh to take it."

Killbuck, who said he had also passed the warning along to Fort Laurens, told McIntosh and Colonel George Morgan, the Indian agent at Fort Pitt, that his Delawares desperately needed munitions. "My young people have no ammunition to defend ourselves, our women and children," Killbuck said. "I therefore beg of you to let me have four casks of powder and lead and flints for our own use."

In late February, Colonel Brodhead at Fort McIntosh and General McIntosh at Fort Pitt wrote significantly different letters to Captain Killbuck and the other Delaware chiefs at Goschachking.

Brodhead acknowledged receiving Killbuck's late January warning of warriors moving against Fort Laurens. Employing native metaphors, he compared these rumors to "the great noise of the birds" and "heavy and dark clouds."

"I am sure the present clouds can be dispelled by some smoke and fire which you will hear of before long," Brodhead said in a February 23 letter.

The colonel encouraged Killbuck "to get a supply of ammunition from our brother, Colonel Gibson, at Tuscarawas, and, if it would suit you, to go and live near that fort for a short time until I can march out an army. I should be much rejoiced because you and him could give each other mutual assistance and be strong against all the bad and foolish people until I come to sweep them away."

By February 20, General McIntosh had requested a reassignment, and Congress had authorized General Washington to appoint someone to succeed him. But McIntosh didn't mention this when he wrote to Killbuck from Fort Pitt two days after Colonel Brodhead did. He reminded the chief that at the September treaty at Pittsburgh, the Delawares had agreed to fight on the American side. "We told you at first in the beginning of the war to sit still and smoke your pipes," he said. "But when these wicked men continued in their mischief and threaten you as well as us, . . . it was time for all the friends of America and Liberty to take up the hatchet for their own sakes with us, as your people did at the last treaty at Fort Pitt."

McIntosh urged the chief "to make a company of your young men to consist of 60 of them" with two captains. The captains should be "the greatest and best warriors among you, . . . to be chosen by your own council and wise men." The United State would provide their provisions and "one suit of clothes every year," and pay them. As soldiers, the Delawares would "take care of our boats and horses . . . carry news, and join us when we go to war to show us the path, find out trails, and anything else that may be required of them."

As winter wore on, Fort Laurens proved increasingly difficult to supply. Pro-British Indians made overland travel so hazardous between Fort Laurens and Fort McIntosh that in early February, General McIntosh attempted to send supplies there by a roundabout route—by water. Although the fort was about 100 land miles west of Pittsburgh, the general sent Major Richard Taylor 150 miles down the Ohio to the mouth of the Muskingum, then another 150 miles up the Muskingum and Tuscarawas.

Taylor took 100 men and several boats laden with supplies: 200 kegs of flour from Pittsburgh and 50 barrels of beef and pork from the garrisons at Fort McIntosh and Fort Henry at Wheeling. Taylor also took "as much whiskey as the (Fort Pitt) commissary . . . can spare," medicine from the fort's hospital, "a blacksmith with his tools, and some iron and steel . . . with any other articles" that the Fort Laurens garrison might need.

At the mouth of the Muskingum, Taylor's boats left the Ohio and turned up the Muskingum, intent on going nearly 90 miles north to Goschachking. They were to reach the Forks of the Muskingum and then sail another 50 miles up the Tuscarawas to Fort Laurens. The boats never got there.

The Delawares at Goschachking certainly knew that the supply boats were headed their way. On February 23, Colonel Brodhead wrote to Killbuck from Fort McIntosh, told him about Taylor's mission, and asked for his assistance. "I shall take it as a strong proof of your friendship if you will send a number of your good men to help and guard Major Taylor up to Tuscarawas."

Records detailing Taylor's exploit don't indicate whether any friendly Delawares rendezvoused with the major. Taylor did, however, encounter enemy warriors. As his boats inched their way up the Muskingum, the major assigned soldiers to walk along the riverbank to flush any hostiles who might be waiting in ambush. One day two men flanking the boats were "killed and scalped by some warriors coming down Muskingum River," McIntosh said. The attack happened as Taylor watched helplessly from a boat.

Around this time, word of Taylor's assignment had reached the Moravian missionaries at Lichtenau. Many pro-British warriors had come into the region, and the missionaries quickly realized the perils that awaited the major and his men.

"We thought Major Taylor in great danger," Heckewelder later advised Colonel Brodhead, "and after considering the matter well with the head men of Goschachking, we concluded it was best for the major to turn back again, and therefore wrote a letter informing him of all circumstances and advising him to turn back again."

Heckewelder added that several days later, "six Mohican warriors, who some days before had stolen two of our canoes and gone down the river in order to cross the Ohio and go to war, came back with two scalps, which they had taken near the mouth of this river."

Taylor failed to get within 100 miles of the fort. The elements were against him. So were the Indians. As McIntosh reported to General Washington on March 12, "He was six days going up about 20 miles of Muskingum River, the waters were so high and stream so rapid . . . As he had above 130 miles more to go, he judged it impossible to relieve Colonel Gibson in time, and therefore returned."

Taylor had sailed out of Pittsburgh around February 8. He returned to Fort Pitt more than a month later. As McIntosh told General Washington on March 12, "I am now happily relieved by the arrival of Major Taylor here, who returned with 100 men and 200 kegs of flour."

If pro-British natives were menacing American troops deep in Indian Country, they were also raiding white settlements near Pittsburgh. On February 26, hostile warriors struck along Turtle Creek in Westmoreland County, some 20 miles east of Fort Pitt. "A scalping party killed and carried off 18 persons—men, women, and children," McIntosh reported. The raid caused "such a panic" among the county's inhabitants that a "great part of them were moving away."

McIntosh said that the attack was "the first mischief done in the settlements since I marched for Tuscarawas" in November. He now considered whether "to rouse the militia, and . . . to retaliate and make an excursion to some Mingo town upon the branch of Allegany River who were supposed to have done the mischief." Instead, the general soon led 500 troops west to relieve Fort Laurens, where, faced with starvation, soldiers in the garrison were boiling, then eating their footwear.

March 1779

# Fort Laurens besieged for 4 weeks

The full moon of March 2 came and went without an attack on Fort Laurens. Nonetheless, in early March, Killbuck learned of "a large body of warriors . . . going up the Tuscarawas" to attack Fort Laurens. He reported to General McIntosh that he sent "some of my wise men to meet them." Together with the three Delawares he had sent to Laurens in late January, these men "after much trouble and by frequent speeches" persuaded the warriors—"consisting chiefly of Shawnees, Wyandots, and Mingos"—to turn back.

They stopped at Goschachking on their way west, and Killbuck addressed them "in hopes of convincing them of the danger they were bringing upon themselves by not receiving the friendship which had so often been offered to them by the 13 united states."

The chief also warned McIntosh that pro-British Indians had infiltrated the region. "There are three parties of warriors between Fort Laurens and Fort McIntosh watching the road, the one of four, the other six and the third of about eight or 10 men," Killbuck said. "There are likewise several parties over the big river (Ohio) for mischief."

Killbuck added that he had "sent a spy" to the towns of the pro-British tribes living along the Sandusky River west of Goschachking. The chief reported all this in a March 13 letter that scholars say was in the handwriting of John Heckewelder.

In a separate letter, this one addressed to Colonel Brodhead, Heckewelder advised that the warriors who turned back "are not at all yet inclined for peace." Writing from Goschachking, the missionary said, "I have heard them this day, as a great part of them are here, they are not at all content that the Delawares stopped them in their undertaking, and say had it not been for them they would have had the fort, and all what is in it by this time."

The missionary emphasized that when the Delawares confronted the enemy warriors, they had already decided "that Fort Laurens should be attacked and to that purpose they were already gathered and had surrounded that post." At this point, the Delawares "delivered speeches to the heads of the warriors, and with some trouble got the enemy to return home again for this time."

By February 28, the day the Delawares sent messengers down the Tuscarawas with warnings for Major Taylor, the hostiles had turned out in force, "there being then at Fort Laurens near 300 assembled," Heckewelder reported.

Conditions at Fort Laurens had steadily deteriorated throughout the winter. For example, on the morning of February 23, hostiles hid in the trees at the edge of the clearing across from the fort. They watched as the gate opened and a wagon came out, followed by 18 soldiers. The men intended to collect horses that had been left outside the fort to graze. As they approached the trees, the soldiers "were fired upon, and all killed and scalped in sight of the fort," McIntosh later reported to General Washington.

Writing about this same incident, Colonel Brodhead identified the Indians as "Mingos, Wyandots, Munsees, Shawnees, and a few of the Delawares who live with the Wyandots." The casualties, Brodhead said, were "a sergeant and 17 men who were sent out to drive in some horses." Sixteen were killed, and two were taken prisoner.

When he thought conditions were safe, Colonel Gibson sent word of the attack to McIntosh. "A messenger . . . who slipped out of Fort Laurens in the night of Sunday the 28th February" reached McIntosh on March 3.

Writing to Washington from Fort Pitt on March 12, McIntosh reported that the garrison had become "so short of provision" and that it was "out of my power to supply them." The general said that he lacked supplies and the manpower to transport what little he had to the Tuscarawas. At any rate, "if I had both, there were no horses to carry it, or forage to feed them."

McIntosh decided to relieve Fort Laurens anyway. To accomplish this, he called on the militia leaders in the Pennsylvania and Virginia counties west of the Alleghenies "to collect all of the men, horses, provision, and forage they could at any price." They were to meet him at Fort McIntosh on March 15, ready to march to the Tuscarawas within a day. "If they would not be prevailed on to turn out, I was determined with such of the Continental troops as are able to march, and all the provisions we have, at all events to go to the relief of Fort Laurens," the general said.

Fort Laurens badly needed rescuing. Half a century later, men stationed there retained vivid memories of the hardship and hunger they had suffered. "The siege lasted some four weeks," recalled Benjamin Biggs, a Virginia

*1776 portrait of General Washington, painted by Charles Willson Peale.*

militiaman. With "provisions exhausted," the soldiers scrounged for scraps of food.

Some became desperate. Even though pro-British warriors might be lurking in the nearby woods, "two of the men in the fort stole out and killed a deer," Biggs said. "and when they returned with it, it was devoured in a few minutes, some not waiting to cook it."

Biggs recalled that "for three or four days (he) had to live on half a biscuit a day." In the days before the relief column arrived, some soldiers "washed their moccasins and broiled them for food, and broiled strips of old dried hides."

March 15 came and went. Despite the urgency, several more days passed before General McIntosh led the relief column out of Fort McIntosh. "I am just setting off for Fort Laurens with about 200 men I have collected of the militia and better than 300 Continental troops from this garrison and Fort Pitt," he told Washington in a March 19 letter.

"Unfortunately," McIntosh said, the soldiers "have not collected horses enough to carry the quantity of provision I intended or would be necessary and as the time will not admit of an hour's delay to wait for any more," he was marching off with as much food as the detachment could carry.

The general said that the region's militia leaders and his own staff agreed that the fort "should not be evacuated by any means if it can possibly be kept and that it may be defended by 100 men if provision cannot be carried for more." In December, McIntosh had left Colonel Gibson at Fort Laurens with a garrison of 172 Continental soldiers. Since then, Indians had killed 20 or more. This left the fort with approximately 150 soldiers. Transferring 50 of these men to other posts would offset the supply shortage at Fort Laurens, if only temporarily.

The hostiles had withdrawn when McIntosh's convoy arrived at the fort in late March. It reached Fort Laurens "late in the evening," veteran Henry Jolly recalled decades later. According to another veteran, Benjamin Biggs, the soldiers inside the fort were so overjoyed that they fired their guns in celebration.

The gunfire frightened the packhorses, many of which ran off into the woods, "scattering flour," Biggs said.

This happened as the column came in view of the fort. "A great part of the flour was lost," Jolly said. "A considerable part of next day was spent hunting horses, and the day following the troops marched for Fort McIntosh."

To be sure, a considerable amount of provision did make its way into the fort. With food suddenly available, "so incautious were many of the men that several made themselves sick with overloading their weak stomachs, and three died in consequence," Biggs said.

General McIntosh said later that when he arrived at Fort Laurens, he told his field officers and militia leaders that he wanted "to proceed to Sandusky and destroy the Wyandot towns, and if we could get any supplies there, proceed farther"—perhaps as far as Fort Detroit—"and if Fortune favored us perhaps finish the matter at once in that quarter by such an unexpected push."

The officers objected. "They were unanimously against it," McIntosh told Washington. They argued "that it was too early in the season, that (a) great part of the road was yet under water, that the little forage we could bring was already exhausted, and the grass would not support our horses yet, and that the small quantity of provision we had, which would serve the garrison of 100 men in Fort Laurens above two months, would only last us 10 or 12 days."

There was an additional reason: The Wyandot towns along the Sandusky were more than 100 miles west of

*General Washington had his headquarters at the Wallace House in present-day Somerville, New Jersey when the Continental Army was nearby at Camp Middlebrook*

Fort Laurens. If they marched to the Sandusky, McIntosh's troops would consume all the provisions, and Fort Laurens "must be evacuated for want of provision whether we succeeded or not." Attacking the Wyandots and abandoning Fort Laurens "probably would unite all the Indians to a man against us, and drive all the inhabitants over the (Allegheny) mountains." A plan to attack Fort Detroit "could at any time be executed with more favorable circumstances while Fort Laurens was kept up and supported in the heart of their country."

The general quickly changed his plan, deposited the provisions at Fort Laurens, and returned to Fort McIntosh and Fort Pitt as rapidly as possible. The trek to Fort Laurens from Fort McIntosh had taken several days, but the return trip took longer. "Our men as well as horses (were) tired, and we were six days coming a journey we made out in little better than three."

Before the general reached Fort McIntosh, the hostiles attacked soldiers gathering wood outside of Fort Laurens.

On March 28, Major Frederick Vernon sent a party of 49 men outside the post to gather wood for the garrison. They didn't see warriors concealed behind a log until the Indians shot and killed two soldiers, "and scalped them before any of the party could come to their assistance."

"The greatest part of the men had picked up their wood and were on their way to the fort" when the attack took place, Vernon said in a report to Colonel Brodhead. "What few men had not got their loads of wood made towards the fort."

"I immediately sent out three Indians to make a discovery how large the party was," the major said. "They returned in a short time, and told me that party was not large, but they had discovered a number of tracks on another point of a ridge, which makes me think there was more than the one party we saw.

"I then sent out a party . . . to bring in the dead bodies. They went to the place where the Indians sat and found four blankets, two green covers and a long knife laying on the top of a laying tree."

"There appeared to be about 10 Indians in that party," Vernon said.

The major, who had taken command of the fort when Colonel Gibson returned to Fort McIntosh a few days earlier, had other news for the colonel: John Heckewelder "was here two days ago, and told me . . . a large party of Indians and some English, with several pieces of artillery, will pay us a visit in a short time. I would be glad to have two pieces of cannon to exchange a shot with them."

Also, "I have received a quantity of corn from Goschachking, but I have not goods that will suit the Indians to satisfy them for bringing it up. I have given a certificate to them for 20 bucks (deer skins), which they expect to be paid to them at Beaver Creek."

When the general reached Fort McIntosh, he found a letter from General Washington waiting for him. McIntosh had been recalled, "you having requested to be relieved" as commander of Fort Pitt and the Western Department,.

Command was passed to one of McIntosh's subordinates. "I have . . . directed Colonel Brodhead to take the command," Washington said.

By April 3, McIntosh was back at Fort Pitt. A little more than three weeks later—on April 27—the general reported for duty at Camp Middlebrook near present-day Bound Brook, New Jersey.

As the year progressed, Washington directed Brodhead to mount a major offensive against the pro-British Senecas living on the Allegheny River high above Pittsburgh. Colonel Brodhead informed Washington, "I have sent orders for the evacuation of Fort Laurens, that the garrison there might be added to the troops already collected for the expedition against the Seneca Country."

On July 16, in ordering Colonel Richard Campbell to prepare to leave Fort Laurens, Brodhead said that the post "will be evacuated as soon as horses can be sent out to bring in the stores, but this must be kept a profound secret; and, as y(our) post may again be occasionally occupied, the works are not to be demolished by our troops."

Hostile warriors remained active around Fort Laurens even as its garrison prepared to depart. "I have just learned that two soldiers have lately been killed at Fort Laurens," Brodhead said on August 4.

The garrison on the Tuscarawas was evacuated on the 1st or 2nd of August, according to Henry Jolly. "I was one of the last that left it," Jolly said. "We arrived at Fort Pitt on the 7th."

# Selective Bibliography

## Books

Darlington, William M., editor. *Christopher Gist's Journals with Historical, Geographical and Ethnological Notes and Biographies of His Contemporaries*. Pittsburgh, J.R. Weldin & Co.,1893

Donehoo, George P. *Indian Villages and Place Names in Pennsylvania*. Baltimore: Gateway Press Inc., 1995.

Hazard, Samuel, editor. *Pennsylvania Archives, Vol. III*. Philadelphia: Joseph Severns & Co., 1853.

———. *Pennsylvania Archives, Vol. V*. Philadelphia: Joseph Severns & Co., 1853.

———. *Pennsylvania Archives, Vol. VI*. Philadelphia: Joseph Severns & Co., 1853.

———. *Pennsylvania Archives, Vol. VII*. Philadelphia: Joseph Severns & Co., 1853.

———. *Pennsylvania Archives, Vol. VIII*. Philadelphia: Joseph Severns & Co., 1853.

Heckewelder, John. *An Account of the History, Manners, and Customs of the Indian Nations, Who Once Inhabited Pennsylvania and the Neighboring States*. Philadelphia: Publication Fund of the Historical Society of Pennsylvania, 1876. (Reprint edition by Arno Press Inc., 1971.)

———. *A Narrative of the Mission of the United Brethren Among the Delaware and Mohegan Indians*. Philadelphia: McCarty & Davis, 1820.

Kellogg, Louise P., editor. *Frontier Advance on the Upper Ohio 1778–1779*. Madison, Wisconsin Historical Society, 1916.

Soderlund, Jean R. *Lenape Country: Delaware Valley Society Before William Penn.* Philadelphia, University of Pennsylvania Press, 2016.

Swift, Robert B. *By Great Rivers: Lives on the Appalachian Frontier.* England, America Through Time, 2019.

Thwaites, Reuben G. and Kellogg, Louise P., editors. *The Revolution on the Upper Ohio, 1775–1777.* Madison, Wisconsin Historical Society, 1908.

———. *Frontier Defense on the Upper Ohio, 1777-1778.* Madison, Wisconsin Historical Society, 1912.

Wallace, Paul A. W. *Indian Paths of Pennsylvania.* Harrisburg: Pennsylvania Historical and Museum Commission, 1971.

Weslager, C.A. *The Delaware Indians.* New Brunswick: Rutgers University Press, 1972.

## Internet resources:

Dictionary.com @ https://www.dictionary.com/
Founders Online @ https://founders.archives.gov/
Google maps @ https://www.google.com/maps/
Internet Archive @ https://archive.org/
Time and Date AS (Timeanddate.com)

# About the Author

John L. Moore of Northumberland is a writer and storyteller whose subjects deal with real people and events in Pennsylvania history.

*The Outposts* is the sixth book in his Revolutionary Pennsylvania Series, which tells the stories of Pennsylvania and Pennsylvanians caught up in the American Revolutionary War. Other books in the series, also works of non-fiction, are *Tories, Terror, and Tea* (2017); *Scorched Earth: General Sullivan and the Senecas* (2018); *1780: Year of Revenge* (2019); *Murder on Killbuck Island* (2020); and *Against the Ice: The Story of December 1776* (2020). Scheduled for publication in 2022, *Border War* will be the seventh book in the series.

*The Outposts* is the author's 14th non-fiction book. Sunbury Press published the eight non-fiction books in his Frontier Pennsylvania Series in 2014.

Mr. Moore has participated in several archaeological excavations of Native American sites. These include the Village of Nain in Bethlehem, Pa.; the City Island project in Harrisburg, Pa., conducted by the Pennsylvania Historical and Museum Commission; a Bloomsburg University dig in 1999 at a Native American site near Nescopeck, Pa.;

and a 1963 excavation of a Native American site conducted by the New Jersey State Museum along the Delaware River north of Worthington State Forest in New Jersey.

Mr. Moore's 46-year newspaper career (1966–2012) included stints as a reporter for T*he Wall Street Journal*; as managing editor of *The Sentinel* at Lewistown, Pa.; as editorial page editor, city editor, and managing editor of *The Daily Item* in Sunbury, and as editor of the *Eastern Pennsylvania Business Journal* in Bethlehem, Pa. He was also a Harrisburg correspondent for *Ottaway Newspapers* in the early 1970s.

A professional storyteller, Moore specializes in historically accurate stories about Pennsylvanians. Wearing 18th-century-style clothing, he often appears in the persona of Susquehanna Jack.

For information about Mr. Moore's storytelling programs and books, please contact:

John L. Moore
552 Queen Street
Northumberland, Pa. 17857
Telephone (570) 556-8096
Email: tomahawks1756@gmail.com